# A Wise and Loving Heart

# Gershom R. Cohn

... in his own words

Celebrating 95 years!

A creative collaboration, comprising his writings sent to his childres and
grandchildren, his family and friends spanning many years.

# Table of Contents

# PHILOSOPHY & SPIRITUALITY

# Preface

To celebrate our Papa's and our Grandpa's (and our Great Grandpa's) 95th birthday, we have chosen to publish the letters he has sent to us over the past 15 years. These words come from his heart and his wisdom. They are the most important legacy we could receive from him: his world view, his ethics, and the meaning of life as he sees it. In writing, he shares himself with us. What a gift. Now we are sharing that gift with you.

We've organized these letters into categories, but Gersh Cohn's thoughts about Love fill all the pages. His philosophy emerges in his self-discovery. His politics emerge from his philosophy. The importance to him of his family is evident in the time and soul searching represented here. He has wanted us to know some of what he has come to know in his life. His humor, his wit, and his wildly imaginative use of language weave throughout his writing.

We believe that Gersh Cohn is an amazing man. You don't have to take it from us. In this written record, his words speak for themselves.

# Family: Invitations, Generosity, and Love

# *Invitation*

Gershom Cohn
510 Blue Jay Place
Sarasota, Florida 34236

This is your invitation to my 100th Birthday Party on May 20th and 21st, 2011. It's true that I'll only be 95 next year, but I want to have the 100th now because: 1) I want to be there and 2) I want to enjoy it.

I'm writing well in advance so you can put my party into your plans for next year. I PROMISE - you'll have a good time. There will be a banquet for family and out-of-town guests on Friday, May 20th and the big party will be Saturday, May 21st at Michael's on East.

Hotel accommodations are excellent. The Lido Beach Resort (on the Gulf) has given me a special rate of $159 in the original building and $199 in the new tower. Their phone number is 941/...... Just mention the Cohn special rate when you call.

Please call me at 941/.... to say yay or nay or maybe.

Best regards,
Gersh

P.S. For many of us, it will be the last time we'll see each other. What a lovely way to say goodbye!

MUCH LOVE -
Gersh

# Ye Olde Patriarch

FROM:          YE OLDE PATRIARCH

TO:             HIS PROGENY, THEIR PROGENY, and assorted relatives and close friends.

RE:             90TH BIRTHDAY OF YOP 3/5/06

I had planned initially to ignore this major birthday and wait for the 100th to celebrate, but there was strong intervention. So – it will be March 2, 3, 4, 5th next year. You may come on the 2nd or 3rd (the big party is Saturday, March 4th) and leave on Sunday the 5th. Reservations have been made for our group at the Holiday Inn on Lido: twin queen, or kind-size bedroom is $224.00, or 254.00 overlooking the beach. Call 1-866-306-5452 and ask for "COHN" reservation for the weekend. I think Francy and Marvin are going to have a "HOSPITALITY" suite, so that no one should starve.

We realize that some will come on the 2nd, others on the 3rd. Plans are being made for both evenings. Please let me know if and when you'll be here

On Sunday (the day of departure) a running breakfast/brunch buffet will be served at 510 Blue Jay Place. For reservations, call 941/....

MUCH LOVE!!!

                         PLEASE, NO PRESENTS!
                         JUST YOUR PRESENCE!

# It Is Mete
# That We Shall Meet
# and Eat and Greet!

Yes and verily, I, Gershom Ralph Cohn, your self-appointed and self anointed PATRIARCH of the Cohn-Melnik-Woolf-Glass-Hechtman clans, do hereby declare the weekend of June 12 - 15, 2003 shall be set aside for a family reunion and a celebration of the 65th Anniversary of your Partiarch and Patriarchess.

This pronouncement is going out to all HEADS OF FAMILY UNITS with the express admonition that it be conveyed to all family members to they will not miss this festive event.

This is the "off-season" so hotel rates wil be quite low – about $90.00 for most rooms and there are reasonable air fares. Southwest flies to Tampa and ATA is great from the Chicago area.

This first meeting will be a mixer given by the hotel at 6:00 p.m., Thursday. Your P & P will host a "Roast and Toast" dinner Friday evening for the family and a few close friends. The main event is a "Re-marriage" and dinner dance Satruday.

Please let me know as soon as possible who is coming from your group – with names and addressses, so they can be contacted individually with further information.

We are looking forward to a wonderful, warm, loving experience for everyone.

# Return from Maine

Your grandmother (or mother) and I just returned from Maine. We had a wonderful visit with Vicki, Howard, and Justin. We saw woods and lakes and woods and ocean and woods and rivers. Everything was fresh and beautiful. One day we went to Campobello and saw the F.D.R. Cottage (37 rooms) and other great views. Campobello is an island, nine miles by three miles, just over the border in Canada.

We also had a nostalgic visit to Haystack where Howard was the executive director before he went into acupuncture and we met lots of people whom we hadn't seen since Howard's 50th, 3 ½ years ago.

Next stop - San Francisco - then in September a visit with the Chicago clan and our family reunion in honor of Sarah and Barbara.

Grandma (mom) says: No cruise for all of us in honor of the 60th anniversary. As you all know, she's the boss and we always abide by her wishes. [HA!! HA!! –Sylvia wrote this...]

Instead, you'll all come here and stay at the Sandcastle Hotel on Lido beach.

Depending on your choice, you'll arrive on March 27th (Friday), 28th (Saturday), or 39th (Sunday),. and leave on the 5th of April (Sunday). [A command from your Pop – again in Sylvia's handwriting.]

On April 3, (Friday), we'll all go to our temple and have the big dinner on Saturday. The size of the party is still indefinite.

I'm sending this information now so you can make your plans now for this momentous event..

MUCH LOVE -

Grandpa (Dad)

# You Stood Up for Me

This missive is for Arlene, Vicki & Howard, David & Jean, Sarah & Barb, Tanya & Will, Loren, Justin, and Molly

You all stood up for me and your M/GM on June 14th and now I want to stand up for you. I think you are all wonderful, and I want you to know that I'm deeply touched by your comments of endearment.

I have written to you many times about love and its importance . . . that there are many kinds of love, all of them good. So it is no surprise to find me ecstatic about the program you presented on Friday the 13th, my lucky day.

For I truly felt bathed in love and overwhelmed by your sincerity and presentation.

All of you (along with Charlie) are our nuclear family. It is a tightly knit, very close, and very loving family. And I take great pride in my part in the creation of this wonderful group. You who have brought in new members have been intuitive enough to choose well. I think it's marvelous that we all have such great respect and love for one another.

I must admit that I'm a sentimental old man, so I cry with joy when I think of my loving family. I love all of you very much!!

Dad/GP

# *Tzedakah*

Dear Arlene, Vicki & Howard, David & Jean,

I was really pleased to get the acknowledgments of your gifts in honor of your mother, and of my 90th birthday.

As you know, I'm big on gifting. I learned to give from my father and I'm happy to see the tradition extended into my offspring.

For me, Tzedakah is the hallmark of our faith. One decent gift is worth 25 prayers in which God is extolled as a supreme being. Giving is loving and whether you are giving of yourself or your wherewithal, you are extending love to your fellow man.

Which reminds me of a new mantra. Try saying LOVE for 15 minutes. It will make you feel better.

And so it is appropriate to end with my usual ending –

MUCH LOVE, Dad

# Yes, There Is a God!!

A number of years ago, a famous editor wrote an article with this title: YES, VIRGINIA, THERE IS A SANTA CLAUS. He theorized that Santa Claus personified the spirit of giving and that he lived in our hearts and minds.

I have paraphrased this title because I, too, feel that an abstract can be very important in our lives and live also in our hearts and minds.

God, for me, is all the goodness, kindness, generosity, good will, justice, equality, and above all, LOVE. God is beauty, strength of character, and our conscience.

I have written before that, in my opinion, man created God, not vice-versa, because we need a God of all those virtues to inspire us and to which we can aspire. "Only God is perfect," a wise person told me and now I believe it. There is no perfection on this Earth, but we always live in the hope that we can be better persons. By that I mean that we can acknowledge our imperfections and be comfortable with them, but we can look at a perfect God and let those values be a guide for our lives.

This month, we celebrate Chanukah and Christmas. The former represents the triumph of good over evil; the latter conveys "peace on earth, good will to man." In both we see man's desire for a better world and a better persona.

So, in the spirit of the season, I wish you a Happy Chanukah and a Merry Christmas. May your personal God smile down on you, give you peace, and lots of love.

MUCH LOVE -
❏ DAD    ❏ G.P.

P.S. - Double distribution is a Chanukah present!

18

# *CH*

CH are the first two letters of Christmas and Chanukah–two wonderful holidays that we celebrate every December. They are wonderful because we celebrate them by giving. Christmas presents are just as important to the donor as well as the recipient. The same is true of Chanukah "gelt." I am sending you some with the hope that you'll put it to good usage.

There is another word that begins with CH, and that is CHEMISTRY! Of course, chemistry is a science, but it has another definition: warm feelings between friends or "good vibes."
We are really talking about loving one another, which is the greatest value in the world. I have written to you a lot about love because it is so important in our lives. Babies can starve without love, and I suppose adults could also.
So here's to Chanukah and Christmas and good chemistry between us. And here's to love–the greatest power in the world!!

MUCH LOVE - Gersh/Dad/GP/GGP/Uncle

December 2009

# Slowdown....
# Depression....
# Recession....

Our brilliant (?) President Bush said it was a SLOWDOWN. The TV and radio announcers carefully use the word RECESSION or DEEP RECESSION. Let's call our economic woe by its true name: DEPRESSION.

In my opinion, it will take a massive effort to bring us out of this depression, and I feel it will last a long time.

But I have a plan! I'm going to beat President Obama to the punch. I'm going to issue my own STIMULUS PLAN.

The enclosed check will help the economy if you spend it wisely. So - go out and help buy our way back to a sound economic situation. I have great confidence that you'll help me.

Also - HAPPY CHANUKAH and/or MERRY CHRISTMAS.

MUCH LOVE -
ME

# It's My Pleasure

...to give you 2% of L.M. This is the holiday season, which I think honors the joy of living with celebration and gift-giving.

I hope that 2007 was a good year for you, and that you and all your family enjoy good health. At my age, health is the #1 concern.

For me, 2007 was not so good. It started with taking the cover off of Sylvia's grave, which hit me hard. It took a whole year to realize that she's never coming back.

Then, I spent too many days in hospital and rehab centers. I hate those places and I'm the worst patient in the world.

But things are looking better now and I have Ruth to share my life. She's wonderful. I wrote recently about the mantra I got from Kali Das: LIFE IS GOOD. I CHOOSE TO BE HAPPY. I came up with one of my own, which also emphasizes the positive: I'M ALIVE AND WELL AND LUCKY AS HELL. ALL IS WELL, YES, ALL IS WELL!!

I hope 2008 is great for you! Thank you for caring for me. You're one of the spokes in my "Wheel of Good Fortune.",

❏ GP    ❏ Uncle Gersh    ❏ Gersh

# Christmas
# & Chanukah

This is a joyous time of the year when we talk about peace on earth, good will to everyone - and the triumph of good over evil.

As for the latter, all we have to do is kvell over the November elections. More of the same - our modern day "Haman" will be gone in two years, and, hopefully, we can have democracy again.

It is only fitting that we celebrate both holidays with gift-giving. It is wonderful to receive gifts and it feels great to give them.

I count as my greatest gift the love all of you bestow upon me. Please accept the enclosed check as a "thank you" for that love.

❏ Dad        ❏ Grandpa        ❏ Uncle        ❏ Friend

# Chanukah Gelt

This is the Chanukah time of the year and with it comes Chanukah GELT! My wife and I are happy to include you in this traditional event, but it comes with two provisions:

~No thank you notes or calls
~ A description of your ingenuity

Thank-yous are superfluous in this case, because we get pleasure from our participation in the annual ritual, and, besides, we know already that you appreciate the gift. However, it is our desire that this C.G. does not go into your regular funds. Instead, do something outrageous with it. Spend it on something you wouldn't ordinarily buy or do.

We have great confidence in your ability, and we'd like you to communicate to us how you spent it or what you spent it on.

❏ Dad
❏ G.P.
❏ Gersh
❏ Friend

P.S. If you can't read this, call for an English translation

P.S.2 We love you!!!

# *2005*

Yes, we have a new year, a fresh start with the opportunity to do better than last year. Perhaps we can be happier this year – or, make someone else happier - which is a noble ambition. I have always felt that one person can make a big difference. Why not you?

If you are superstitious (as I am) you'll love 2005, as the total of all these numbers is 7. That is my lucky number, so maybe the year will be a good one for me. To finish the year is an excellent goal and, above all, perhaps George W. Bush might make a good decision ... or two.

The enclosed checks represent the dividends that have been promised. The good news is that barring unseen and unfortunate circumstances, these dividends should remain constant for a long time.

2004 brought us Maxwell Thomas Rubin and 2005 will bring some sort of a Stenhouse. Great! Your M/GM is stabilized, and, hopefully, will stay that way. I'm certain that acupuncture has helped immensely. Maybe 2005 will be good for all of us.

MUCH LOVE -

Dad/GP

# E.J.'s Contract

Between Esmeralda Juanita Walker [EJ] and Gershom Ralph Cohn [Gersh]

1.      Four-day work week for EJ – Mon., Wed., Thurs., & Fri.–from 11 AM to the end of dinner hour for $500.00 a week. This salary gives EJ a strong base for her living expenses, plus money for Corky and the use of her car, as it is necessary

2.      Any other work during the week will be compensated at the rate of $12.50 per hour

3.      24-hour day will be $150.00

4.      Any gifts or bonuses will be at the discretion of Gersh

5.      Gersh promises to try hard to overlook EJ's propensity to control everything and attempt to present his views to her

6.      Contract negotiations may be reopened any February 29th between the hours of 5 and 8 AM.

Signed, this 17th day of May, 2004

EJ_____    Gersh _____


NOTE: check EJ's middle name here.

# Love Is the Key

It was Yom Kippur Eve and Justin and I were in the front row in the Temple Beth Israel on Longboat Key. As we rose for the first silent prayer, a voice said to me "Love is the key to happiness."

I have written a lot about love... the prime ingredient in everyone's life... the strong base for all religions... the most powerful, dynamic force in the world... but this concept that love is a key is quite different.

Why a key? And, what does a key do? Of course, it turns a lock. And why the lock? Is something locked in... or locked out?

Then there's happiness... certainly a variable and subjective word. I have found personal happiness when I turned the key in several locks and came to realize how deeply I love my unique, wonderful wife. This love is reciprocated and our former combativeness has disappeared. I know a man with few friends and who donates virtually nothing. Yet he's happy counting his millions as he plans to line his coffin with his stocks and bonds.

My greatest wish for all of you is that you use the key of love to open the doors which are concealing deep, dark secrets. Your understanding of your inner conflicts can bring understanding and, with it, the peace and happiness that you deserve.

Lovingly,

❑ G.P.   ❑ Dad

# LECSIP

Before I start today's missive, I want to comment on the wedding. It was wonderful!! But more wonderful was the mini "Cohn Family Reunion!" It was such a pleasure to see all of you in person, and especially our newest members: Will, Patty, and Stacy.

I must say that the wedding of Tanya and Will was quite moving and inspired me to write this piece. The "memoirs" begin again in September.

Many of you know that I do the "Jumble" every day. I use my C.C.T.V. and I truly enjoy it. Most of the words are easy, but occasionally I am stymied. So it was with LECSIP. I'm sure that some of you know what it is. Many times the proper juxtaposition of letters just falls into place. After a long time and lots of rearrangement of letters, I found the answer. It's a word not used in normal conversation – SPLICE.

Then I remembered the meaning of the word. It's used primarily with rope. When they splice it together, weaving all the strands together, it becomes like one rope.

My wife and I were spliced 64 years ago. There has been a lot of tugging, but the splice has held. In fact, it's stronger than ever.
As I look around our closely-knit family, I observe that we all take our splicing seriously. There's David and Jean, Vicki and Howard, Tanya and Will, Barb and Sarah, and the new ones: Justin and Stacy, Loren and Patty. And, of course, my sisters and their mates.

I'm proud of all of us who are spliced so well, because this bespeaks of commitment and lovingness. Didn't I hear someone say that love is the greatest value in life???

MUCH LOVE–

Dad/GP

# Live for the Moment

Occasionally I have dreams that are vivid and clear. I had one recently that bears discussion.

I was talking with a 13 year old boy and I found myself remonstrating with him: "Live for the moment," I almost shouted. He seemed visibly impressed.

My good friend Saul Rosenberg, an excellent psychologist, says that everyone in your dreams is you. So the 13 year old boy was me, and 13 is the Bar Mitzvah age. In Jewish tradition this is the age when a boy becomes a man. In the dream the boy couldn't wait until he was older and that's why I yelled at him.

Then I asked myself if I was concerned about the future of my sick wife and myself. The answer was "yes," and it's understandable, considering our age.

So, I was talking to myself, as well as to the boy. Deep down inside is an intelligence that is serving me well. I'm going to "live for the moment" and let the future play out as it happens. What will be will be.

I know we'll all live for the moment next June. I don't think that's too far away for the "moment" classification.

To conclude this rather rambling piece, my best advice is to live for the moment, with a clear concept of the past as a guide for improvement, and plan carefully for the future so you can continue to live for the moment as the moments occur.

MUCH LOVE -

Dad/GP

# "Wunnerfull, Wunnerfull, Wunnerfull"

Lawrence Welk, an old time Hungarian band leader, would say that to his singer, trio, or quartet when they performed well.

I believe strongly that "wonderful is a wonderful word" and should be used instead of that NON-WORD - perfect. As you all know by now, there is no perfection.

For example, we do live in a wonderful world (far from perfect) with many wonderful advantages.

I happen to live in a wonderful house with a wonderful wife and a wonderful dog and we have a wonderful driver.

I am writing to my three wonderful children, five wonderful grandchildren, and the three wonderful additions to our family.

MUCH LOVE FROM YOUR WONDERFUL

❏ G.P.     ❏ Dad

# A Very Rich Man???

When I was going to visit Vicki and Howard recently, I sat next to a very interesting man on the flight from Atlanta to Bangor. He was in his mid-60's and on his way to Camden to vacation with some friends for a week.

We became quite confidential in our conversation. He was more so, as I plied him with questions in my usual direct manner.

This is what I learned about him. He was the right-hand man of the CEO of Holiday Inn Corp., and in that capacity visited with and entertained royalty throughout the world. He made money with Holiday Inn and became a big investor in young companies. One of his plums was Federal Express, which went up and split many times. He has zillions of shares (he would not tell me how many) with an average cost of six cents per share. The price is now well over $100.00 per share.

One of his present ventures is a huge interest in a company which provides a service to banks. Bank of America is one of its largest clients. The company is not on the stock market yet, as its volume is only $65,000,000.00 a year. When it does reach $100,000,000.00, it will be an I.P.O. (initial public offering) and he'll make more millions.

These are just two examples of his holdings. He also has a large home in Memphis, where he lives, plus homes in Key West, Florida and California.

So, on the surface, he's living the American Dream: great financial success, rising from a poor family to the royalty of money.
However, he worked so hard to become rich that he didn't have time to have a family. He has no wife, no children, and no grandchildren. Thus, in my opinion, he's a poor man, not a rich one.
By contrast, when I count my assets, I estimate the value of your M/GM/GGM as ½ billion, and all the rest of you - including the wonderful additions that you brought in to the family, as another ½ billion. This makes me a billionaire!!!

In conclusion, there are several points I want to make:

I. Money is quite important, but only up to a certain point. Beyond that it becomes a question of how much to give to charity.

II. There are many other considerations than money to make a well-rounded and happy life.

III. The greatest value in the world is LOVE! It is the chief ingredient for a happy life, and I thank God (whoever she might be) that we have so much love in our family.

As for Mr. Rice, the wealthy man I met on the plane, he might be happy piling up more and more millions, but that is his choice. Remember you all have many choices as we go through life.

MUCH LOVE,

❏ Dad,   ❏ GP,   ❏ GGP

# Speaking of Alliteration

Speaking of alliteration (who was??) our pleasant peripatetic Polish princess (EJ–who else?) prepared for us a peasant pot pie for our pleasure.

It was almost perfect and it was particularly plentiful. EJ is truly a powerful person.

This is Sunday AM 4/25/04 and I write this light-hearted afterthought because of the alliteration in Chapter XXI. But my heart is not light. It's heavy because this morning I reluctantly concluded that your beautiful, wonderful M/GM is now in Phase II of her disease, and I realize how terminal it is.

MUCH LOVE–Dad/GP

# What Is a Neurotic Person?

He (or she) is a human being, period! To quote a famous man "everyone is neurotic - it's just a question of degree." I won't tell you his name, but the initials are G.R.C.

Howie and Vicki are off to India next week to visit the country and to study Indian Buddhism. Justin starts a three-month study in California exploring Tibetan Buddhism. What are they seeking to learn? What do we seek to learn from our psychologists and psychiatrists? In broad terms: TRUTH.

We want to learn the truth about ourselves, our feelings, the great truth of the universe, and why do we all become introspective at times? Because - I don't know who said this, but - "The truth shall set you free."

The greatest truth I have learned is that the most positive, dynamic force in the world is love. If we love ourselves and our fellow man, we rate as decent human beings.

I love you all very much!

G.P. - Dad

# Photo of the Birds

The enclosed photo of the birds was taken on our lanai. The big bird (I think she's a dove) built a nest in our Swedish ivy which is in the corner next to the kitchen.

Ann got this shot just a day or two before they all left, as I watered the plant shortly after and they were gone.

Now, another bird is sitting on two eggs in a begonia plant on the lanai. It is hanging on the arm that extends next to the door leading to the dining room. She flies away when I water, but then returns.
This also happened before with another begonia. I guess the birds knew we are animal lovers.

GM and I leave May 7th for Decatur and Chicago. At the latter, we'll go to Jay Hechtman's daughter Jennifer's wedding. We'll get a chance to visit with Arlene, Sarah, and Barb.

Tanya and Loren have written me. It was great to hear from two of the recipients of the monthly epistles. But I'm not complaining!

MUCH LOVE from G.M–G.P.–Dad–and Me

# To Thine Own...

Last month my youngest grandchild, Molly, became 21 years old. I couldn't think of any aphorism or adages to send her - such as "the harder I work, the luckier I get" or "everything in moderation, including moderation." So I dug deep into my memory bank and came up with these comments by Polonius in "Hamlet":

To thine own self be true -
And it follows, as the night the day,
Thou canst not be false to any man.

She liked that and I do too because the inference is to LOVE YOURSELF, which I have been writing you to do for many years.

As I think about President Obama's recent wonderful speech to the Muslim world, his overall plea was for everyone to try to love one another with compassion and consideration.

He ended his speech with a quote from our Jewish ancestors (which has been incorporated into almost every religion): LOVE THY NEIGHBOR AS THYSELF! He also quoted from the Koran and the Christian Bible the same wonderful advice which was worded a bit differently.

I also felt that he was telling the world that war is useless and doesn't really decide or improve things. Thus, the only way out of all these ugly messes the world is in, is to emphasize the positive, not the negative, and we should stop hating and start loving.

So - out of all this discussion comes a modernized version of Polonius' speech:
To thine own self be loving,
And it follows, as the night the day,
Thou cannot be hurting and hating
Of your fellow man or woman.

P.S. All this cogitation has created a new "bon mot":
LOVE is the balm that calms the spirit and cleanses the soul.

# Thank You Israel

I grew up in small towns in Illinois, where there wasn't overt anti-Semitism, but a tacit understanding that Jews were second-class citizens. And the societal pressure made me believe it.

But something wonderful happened in 1948: The State of Israel came into being and I immediately became a FIRST-CLASS CITIZEN!

During these past 60 years of Israel's existence, I have been so proud of all the accomplishments of Israel. And I've never lost my status as a first-class citizen.

THANK YOU ISRAEL!
Gersh Cohn

# It's True! I'm a Jew

It's true! I'm a Jew who, at age 92, did stew and stew anew, so you too might review these words, old and new, all ending with OOH:

| | | |
|---|---|---|
| ADIEU | ANEW | AGUE |
| ASKEW | AVENUE | BALLYHOO |
| BAMBOO | BARBEQUE | BLEW |
| BLUE | BOO | BOO-HOO |
| BOOBALOU | BREW | CANOE |
| CARIBU | CARIMISU | CASHEW |
| CLUE | COCKATOO | COCK-A-DOODLE-DOO |
| DOO | COO | COO-COO |
| CREW | CURFEW | DEBUT |
| DÉJÀ VU | DEW | DO |
| DOO-DOO | DUE | EMU |
| EWE | FEVER | FEW |
| FLEW | FONDUE | GNU |
| GOO | GOO-GOO | GREW |
| GURU | HAIRDO | HEBREW |
| HUE | HULLABALOO | IGLOO |
| IMBUE | IMPROMPTU | INTERVIEW |
| INTO | JEW | KNEW |
| LIEU | LOO | LULU |
| MALIBU | MENU | MILIEU |
| MISCONSTRUE | MISCUE | MOO |
| NEW | OOH | OVERSHOE |
| OVERVIEW | PEW | POO-POO |
| QUEUE | RENDEZVOUS | RENEW |
| RESCUE | RESIDUE | REVIEW |

| | | |
|---|---|---|
| RUE | SCREW | SHOE |
| SLEW | SPEW | STREW |
| SUE | TABOO | TATTOO |
| THREW | THROUGH | TO |
| TOO | TRUE | TUTU |
| TWO | VALUE | VENUE |
| VIEW | VIRTUE | VOODOO |
| WATERLOO | WHEW | WHO |
| YAHOO | YOU | ZOO |
| ZULU | | |

There must be more – please send them to me.

LOVE—Gersh/Dad/GP

# Sylvia Is Gone

And I am in mourning because I have suffered the greatest loss of my life. She was my lover, my friend, and my confidante. We were like one... it was either Gersh and Syl or Syl and Gersh.

However, my bereavement is ameliorated by my fantastic family and wonderful friends. So many people have called, sent cards, and sent food, flowers and contributions in her honor.

You are in the latter category and I want you to know how much I appreciate your gift. Thank you! Thank you! Thank you!

In my opinion, giving is our greatest Jewish tradition, and Sylvia always joined me in my philanthropy and my philanthropic endeavors.

Thanks again, and please don't worry about me. I have the strength and desire to pick up the pieces and work toward the creation of a new life.

Best regards and love -

Gersh

# *Worry*

Dear children and grandchildren,

If you are inclined to worry about me – don't! Your mom's death was a bitter blow to me, far harder inside than on the surface. But, I'm finally coming around to accept reality.

This, of course, means that you have to play with the cards that are dealt you. It's so important to count your blessings and be grateful for everything you have. My next motto is, "All is well – so what the hell."

Charlie and I are enjoying our early morning walks, and I play bridge four times a week and the food is very good here. E. J. is doing a good job.

Recently, I went out with a very nice lady and I plan to see her again. Nothing may come of it, but, if not, I'll look for another one. Another case in the acceptance of reality.

David, Vicki and Arlene will be visiting me in May and June. If any of you grandchildren want to enjoy some nice <u>warm</u> weather this summer, come on down!

MUCH LOVE –

Dad/GP

# Hope

"Hope is eternal in the human breast" and I might add the mind also. We live in hope no matter how gloomy the situation.

Today, the world is in a mess. Along with terrorism, we have wars, starvation, and economic depression.

Yet, we have hope. We hope that Obama can lead us back to our leadership position, and world-wide prosperity, with no more terrorism.

My personal hope for the New Year is that Howard can recover and that all of us can live in good health. At my age, health is the #1 priority, but I also have hopes for an economic recovery.

I hope all of you have a great 2009!

MUCH LOVE -
Dad, GP, GGP

# *Life is Good!*

I am proud of all my grandchildren and I "KVELL" at all their wonderful accomplishments. I am particularly impressed at the moment by Loren's activity: at age 41, he has returned to college and is getting a Master's Degree in Education. And, he's doing it well.

One of his assignments was to write a letter to someone, telling him why he loved him. Loren chose me.

I am sending you a copy of this letter because I think he did it so well. I give him A++. Stan said it would be fitting to read this letter at my memorial service. He's right! So I hereby commission Loren to read it at that time.

MUCH LOVE,

❏ Dad, ❏ GP, ❏ GGP

# Oatmeal
# à la Gershom

1. Place 2 tablespoons of raisins in the bowl
2. Put 3 heaping tablespoons of Quick Oats on top of the raisins
3. Slice a small or medium-size banana over the raisins
4. Cover all with ½ glass of water
5. Cook in microwave for 5 minutes
6. Cover with 1 full glass of milk

And then say "thank you" to the genius who made this recipe.

--Dad/GP

# Oatmeal (revisited)

I'm sure that all of you have committed my famous recipe for "Oatmeal Gershom" to memory and have used it many times. So that you might enhance your enjoyment of this great delicacy, I offer the following improvements: (1) use a large banana instead of a medium size, and (2) add one more tablespoon of raisins.

True Story???

A man and his wife were reminiscing about their life together as they celebrated their 50th Anniversary. He said, "Dear, I am in a mellow mood and I want to confess to you that I have left our marital bed on several occasions. But I want you to tell me about your indiscretions. I promise–I won't be angry."

She replied, "I'm so glad this came up. Now I won't feel guilty anymore. There were three times. The 1st–remember when you were starting in business and the banker wouldn't give you the loan? And the next day he changed his mind. The 2nd–remember when the IRS man wanted to charge you $50,000 in penalties?And the next day there were no penalties, just the tax you didn't pay. The 3rd time–remember when you wanted to get in that fancy golf club and you were 38 votes shy . . . ."

I'm certain that you'll recognize this story to be an example of mathematical skill.

MUCH LOVE

   –GP/Dad

# Philosophy and Spirituality

# There's no such thing as

# PERFECTION!

# *Perfection*

Please go to the dictionary and look up PERFECT and PERFECTION. When you find them, take a thick black pen and cover them both with ink.

You see, my loved ones, nothing is perfect, and there is no perfection. It has taken me eighty-three years and a lot of introspection to come to these wonderful conclusions.

I say "wonderful" because it's a great relief to know you don't have to be perfect, nor do you have to have perfection. You'll be able to accept and love yourself exactly as you are and everyone else also.

Look in the mirror and say, "I'm an imperfect person in an imperfect world," and then grin!

We have all been infected with the perfection virus, which has been handed down from generation to generation. I even chose a perfectionist wife because she is like my perfectionist mother.

The chains are strong and hard to break. Let's all try real hard... and live happier lives.

SEE YOU IN ALASKA!!

❏ Dad   ❏ G.P.

I love you all - exactly as you are!!!

# Feelings

In Temple, on Yom Kippur, I was shocked and dismayed when the Rabbi read the list (from A to Z) of the "sins" we were confessing and asking forgiveness for.

As I review this list (see attached copy of the prayer book), I found only four that could possibly be called ACTIONS. All the rest were FEELINGS! A natural question is, "Why should we feel guilty about our feelings?"

My theory is that the promulgators of the Judeo-Christian Ethic, in their zeal to build a conscience within all their followers so that everyone will want to be a good person, went too far. They made us feel guilty of our feelings as well as our acts. This judgmental internal guilt has been passed on from generation to generation.

Thus, we find billions of dollars spent every year for Aspirin, Advil, Aleve, Tylenol, etc., etc. As people attempt to repress the so-called "bad feelings" they not only get headaches, but all kinds of psychosomatic pains and many diseases. The word disease is really dis-ease.

I dreamt I was having a conversation with my mother. We discussed many things, and then, out of the blue, she said, "Treasure your feelings."

I have pondered this profound wisdom many times and I have concluded that it means two things. First, our feelings are an integral part of us and, more importantly, they define us as human beings.

So, listen to the words of wisdom from your grandmother (and great-grandmother). Treasure your feelings and never, never, never feel guilty about them.

MUCH LOVE -

❏ Dad    ❏ G.P.

# Maxim-ize Your Life

A collection of thoughts from a lifetime of observing the human condition

By Gershom R. Cohn - Ye Olde Filosofer

Love is the most powerful force in the world.
There are many different kinds of love–all of them wonderful!
Hate is a killer – externally and internally.

AUDEN: We must love each other or die!

AUDEN REVISED: We must love each other or live in a constant state of conflict and antagonism.

A happy person is one who can handle the exigencies of life.

There is external happiness, but real happiness comes from inside.

THOREAU: The masses live lives of quiet desperation.

THOREAU REVISED: Most people live lives of quiet desperation.

The Happy Medium is not a joyous spiritualism. But it is a wonderful guideline for a "well-balanced" life.

Everything in moderation–even moderation.

There is no perfection–only wonderful.

I am counting my blessings and loving myself. (This is a MANTRA–repeat 100 times or more.)

Everyone is neurotic–it's just a question of degree.

Humankind is an animal with a marvelous brain, and a conscience that has been warped by societal pressures and neurotic parents.

Gratefulness leads to equanimity.

Acceptance of pain is the first step towards its diminution.

Early to bed and early to rise. makes a man feel he needs two wives.

Feelings are problems from the cradle to the grave.

NEVER, NEVER feel guilty about your feelings.

Words can hurt, words can heal, words can inspire, words can destroy. Choose your verbiage carefully.

Acceptance of the status quo is the first step for change.

Forgiveness is the height of lovingness.

The burden of the Judeo-Christian ethic is too heavy for most people to bear.

Withdrawal and rejection create constipation of the body and the mind.

Repressing anger is like swallowing a time bomb.

"Religion is the conservation of values," - HOEFFDING. Thus, God is an abstract concept–the embodiment of Love, Truth, Honesty, Justice, Kindliness, Generosity, Compassion, Understanding, and Beauty.

Religion is too dogmatic and has too much dogma. It is losing followers because it is too rigid and refuses to change.

Early primitive people had two major drives: food and sex. Modern sophisticated people have two major drives: food and sex.

Life is like good theater. There is comedy and tragedy, sex and murder, joy and sorrow. Enjoy the play!

Everything we have is borrowed, including our time on this earth. We arrive with nothing and we leave with nothing.

A person is not even a blip in the eons of time.

Action relieves anxiety.

Live in love-not hate.

Live in the present-not the past.

Live in reality-not fantasy.

To my children and grandchildren:

I have written to you monthly for several years, giving you fatherly and grandfatherly advice-as well as my views on many subjects. Much of this is embodied in this month's missive. I do not ask that you agree with me on all my thoughts. But-I am hopeful that they are a stimulus for your own reflections. Much of my thoughts are about our feelings because, in my opinion, this is the area of discontent, misunderstanding, and downright lies that have been inadvertently passed on from generation to generation for thousands of years.

Get out of the rut!

MUCH LOVE, DAD/GP

# Humankind is an Animal

In my "Maxim-ize Your Life" I wrote: "Humankind is an animal with a magnificent brain and emotions that are warped by pressures from society and neurotic parents.

As I recalled vivid experiences during my life in Gillespie, I thought of two experiences which I chose to leave out, but which illustrate the concept of warped emotions so clearly.

FIRSTLY–One evening my father took me to the local theater for what was called a "Father and Son Night." There were hundreds of men and their sons in attendance. The speaker was an evangelistic preacher and he talked interminably on his subject, "The Evils of Masturbation." The only thing I remember is his point that it would grow hair in the palms of your hands.

SECONDLY–One evening when I was 12 or 13, we drove to Edwardsville to visit Joe and Ceil Hochman. The latter was my Dad's cousin. Their daughter, Shirley, was my age, and she decided that I needed some sex education. At that point I was very retarded in the area and she was quite advanced.

She took me into the bathroom where I learned about her mother's monthly experience and then we went outside in our car. She wanted to do something which I couldn't quite understand and nothing happened. There might have been some kissing – I can't remember.

But here's the sad part: She told her Aunt Bertha about it, and big mouth Bertha told my parents who promptly raised hell with me, because I was painted as the aggressor.

I use these two horrible examples to illustrate how emotions can become warped and GUILT and SHAME become (understandably) part and parcel of a person's psyche. I'm certain everyone can relate similar experiences, because we have failed to acknowledge our real persons and deal with it accordingly. Most everyone has been taught the "DENIAL SYNDROME," which, of course, is painful.

# The Case of the Judeo-Christian Ethic

JUDGE: If you are ready, proceed.

STATE'S ATTORNEY: Thank you, your honor. The state intends to prove that the Judeo-Christian ethic has gone too far in establishing "conscience" in its followers. There is a lack of differentiation between ACTIONS and FEELINGS.

I submit exhibit A for your perusal. This is a listing of all the sins Jews atone for on Yom Kippur. It is a copy of their prayer book and, as you can see, it is a listing of sins from A to Z.

I shall not discuss each so-called "sin" but I want to point out that only four are checked that could remotely be called ACTIONS. The rest are just FEELINGS, which I claim are unstoppable and not punishable. Your honor, have you ever punished anyone for having feelings?

Now, let's take a look at Catholicism, the extreme wing of the Christian faith. All their nuns, priests, bishops, cardinals, and the Pope are celibate. What kind of message are they sending to their parishioners and especially to the Catholic children? They are saying wordlessly that sexuality and fornication is sinful and that all feelings of sexuality are to be decried and repressed.

Your honor, you and I and every other human being are mortal and have basic animal instincts and other human feelings. We cannot deny them. When we try to repress our feelings, we cause great harm to our bodies, because our mind and body are so closely related. Many professional therapists believe this repression and revulsion of our feelings cause headaches, stomach aches, tension... even diseases such as diabetes, cancer, high blood pressure, high cholesterol, etc., etc.

Your honor, please consider all of the facts I have presented when you make your decision.

JUDGE: Are you ready for the defense?

DEFENSE ATTORNEY: Yes, your honor. These are serious charges and should be viewed from a larger concept of the Jewish and Christian faiths and their purposes. I feel it would be difficult for anyone to disagree that religion is a conservation of values, that its main purpose is to inculcate their followers with these values, and to lead wholesome, healthy lives.

I will agree that, in so doing, they have built a conscience in every Jew and every Christian, so that they will be exemplary citizens without the threat of legal punishment.

I will admit that, in their zeal, the original promulgators of religious practices might have gone too far and made their followers feel guilty of their feelings as well as their acts. But sometimes we have to go too far to get the desired results. And, I think your honor will agree that the Jewish and Christian people who truly believe in their faith have become good citizens.

JUDGE: Thank you both for presenting your cases well. I shall consider all aspects of this most interesting case and deliver a verdict in ten days.

TEN DAYS LATER

JUDGE: This is a case with no precedent, which adds to the difficulty of arriving at a proper decision. I recognize the fact that the Jewish religion is over five thousand years old and the Christian religion is over two thousand years old. Perhaps that fact is at the heart of this controversy, as there has been virtually no change in their practices in all these years. I must admit that the defense made an excellent point when it pointed out the excellent citizenship of the followers of both faiths. But then I have to agree with the State Attorney that they pay a huge price for repression of their feelings.

Thus, I must decide that the Judeo-Christian ethic is guilty as charged, but not guilty of major overall goals. Tradition is wonderful, but should be modified if it is harmful.

I charge all leaders of both Judaism and Christianity to reexamine the doctrines of each religion which have been so sacrosanct for too long, and I strongly urge them to effect the changes necessary for modern day living and the emotional health of their people. This will not be easy, for dogma is dogmatic and we all resist change. But it is imperative that it be done.

NEXT CASE!!

EXHIBIT A

"We all have committed offenses; together we confess these human sins:

The sins of arrogance, bigotry, and cynicism; of deceit and egotism, flattery and greed, injustice and jealousy.

Some of us have kept grudges, were lustful, malicious, or narrow-minded.

Others were obstinate or possessive, quarrelsome, rancorous, or selfish.

There was violence, weakness of will, xenophobia.

We yielded to temptation and showed zeal for bad causes."

CONCLUDING SERVICE

'We all have committed offenses; together we confess these human sins:

The sins of arrogance, bigotry, and cynicism; of deceit and egotism, flattery and greed, injustice and jealousy.

Some of us have kept grudges, were lustful, malicious, or narrow-minded.

Others were obstinate or possessive, quarrelsome, rancorous, or selfish.

There was violence, weakness of will, xenophobia.

We yielded to temptation, and showed zeal for bad causes.

# Why Two Missives on the Same Subject?

I wrote the courtroom piece first and didn't like it. As I was ready to tear it up, I decided to send it to Vicki for her appraisal. In the meantime, I wrote the second one.

Since Vicki liked the first one because of its different approach to the subject, I decided to send them both.

Perhaps the double barrel will make you more cognizant of the "feeling" problem and its solution.

HAPPY BIRTHDAY TO OUR ONE & ONLY LOREN!

Loren is enjoying a big birthday - he's 35 years old and he has Patty to share his joy.

Grandma (mother) and I decided that starting with Loren's major birthday, we would gift $5,000 to all the children and grandchildren

So - you have something to look forward to - unless we go broke. Justin is next, and lord knows he'll need it!!!

MUCH LOVE -

❏ G.P.    ❏ Dad

# The New Ten Commandments

Attached is the final revised copy of the New Ten Commandments.

I want you to know that this is an important contribution on my part, as it is a compilation and distillation of my works for the last fifteen years, and my thoughts about religion that I developed over the last 64 years.

In 1936 I took a course in "The Philosophy of Religion." The author of the text we used believed strongly that religion was a conservation of values. I agree. But my ruminations were all about God. Who or what is God? Did he create man or did man create him? I have concluded that the latter is true.

A greater consideration is: why were God and religion created? I may be wrong, but I think I have the answer: to build a conscience within us so that we'll be good. In accordance with this line of thought, the Ten Commandments have a lot of "Thou shall not." These are negative commandments.

GOD IS LOVE - a tremendous, powerful force that is greater than anything in the world. I firmly believe that. For me, God portrayed as the man in the sky who will send lots of lightning to destroy us if we're bad is just another way to make people be good.

Note that the New Ten Commandments are all positive and all about LOVE. This, of course, reflects my belief that God is love.

When I think of lovingness, I think of my parents. It's true that they harmed Francy, Estelle and me by passing on to us psychological factors that were taught to them. But it is also true that they gave us stability and character by their lovingness. I feel that their love has been passed on to their children, grandchildren, and great-grandchildren.

We are a loving family! Of course, we have our differences, but somehow we manage to work things out. The basic thread of our continuity and congeniality is love.

How do I wind up my revelations of my intimate thoughts?

It is easy! I want you all to know that I am a loving man and that I love all of you immensely.

Dad
GP


P.S. Gershom was the son of Moses, who brought the original Ten Commandments from the top of Mount Sinai. Thus, it is fitting that I bring the new Ten Commandments down from the top of Mount Sarasota!!

## THE NEW TEN COMMANDMENTS

I     LOVE THYSELF EXACTLY AS YOU ARE
You are wonderful! No one is, has been, or will be
exactly like you.

II     LOVE THY MATE
Don't forget he or she is your best friend.

III     LOVE THY FATHER AND THY MOTHER
They did the best they could for you.

IV     LOVE THY CHILDREN AND THY
GRANDCHIL DREN
They really, really need your unconditional love.

V     LOVE THY FELLOW MAN
Ninety-five percent (95%) are decent.
It's only five percent (5%) that cause all the trouble.

VI     BE LOVING, BE GENEROUS
I am convinced that Tzedakah (giving) is the
cornerstone of Judaism.
To give of yourself or your money is a true act of love.

VII     LIVE IN THE PRESENT, NOT THE PAST
Yesterday is history, tomorrow is a mystery, and today
is a gift. That's why they call it the present.

VIII     USE "WONDERFUL" instead of "PERFECT"
There is NO perfection, but there's plenty of wonderful!

IX     BE GRATEFUL
You have a lot to be thankful for. So – do it!

X     BE ACCEPTING
Accepting everything as it is leads to joy and happiness!

# I Thank God

Yesterday I made a prayer which I feel is quite meaningful. It goes like this: I THANK GOD I'M HERE TO ENJOY THIS MOMENT!

As most of you know, I feel that God is one of the most nebulous words in the dictionary. I have always felt that God is an abstract, with LOVE and all its ramifications as the best definition of God.
And, at my age, or any age, really, I am thankful that I'm still alive. Many times when I'm greeted at a party with the oft-repeated, "It's good to see you," I reply, "It's good to see anybody." For me, with my sight, that's a double entendre.

I think I've told you this before, but it has bearing on this prayer. It's the story about the psychiatrist who had to deal with two boys–one an optimist, the other a pessimist. He put the optimist in a room filled with manure, and the pessimist in a room filled with wonderful toys. After fifteen minutes he went into the room of the optimist and found him digging like crazy in the manure. He said, "With all this shit, there must be a pony here." Then he went to the room of the pessimist, whom he found sitting on the floor saying sadly, "None of these toys is any good."

I feel we all live with a little pessimist inside who just isn't happy because he or she can't have perfection. If you tell him or her to enjoy the moment you are saying, "Hey, things aren't perfect–but they're pretty damn good."

I'm offering you this prayer with the hope that you'll consider using it, and that it will be as helpful to you as it has been to me. It can also be used effectively as a mantra. MUCH LOVE–Dad/GP

# On Copulation

I feel great satisfaction as I sense your anticipation of my delineation of my observations on copulation and/or fornication. I sincerely hope there will be no confusion.

## I. PROPAGATION
There are many who feel that copulation is only for increasing the population. The Anglicans firmly believe that Mary was, is, and always will be, a Virgin. They are also certain that nuns, priests, and bishops are celibate. They also believe in the tooth fairy.

## II. PARTICIPATION
This category is much akin to Propagation. A few generations ago, women (to a great extent) felt that copulation was a duty and their participation was a resolution of their marital obligation. Despite the sexual revolution, there are still those whose participation is more as bystanders.

## III. RECREATION
This is the greatest group whose motivation is solely sexual satisfaction. It usually winds up with great exultation and vocalization. A recent survey showed that French people hold the record for frequency of fornication, or gratification and satisfaction.

## IV. MASTURBATION
This is performed by one or two individuals to bring compensation without condemnation. Some who work in pairs do not feel that it is fornication because there is no penetration. They are called "Clintonians." Remember Bill with his finger pointing at you, saying "I never had sex with that woman!"

## V. ELEVATION
This is the highest form of copulation. It is maturation to the realization that love is the most important factor in the equation. The dictionary defined copulation as "joining together." Thus, the real feeling of oneness and togetherness is the ELEVATION to the highest form of copulation.

The sensation of exhilaration is just and fair compensation for your completion of the cooperation that is needed for this relation-ship.

A noted psychiatrist once said, "Sexuality is a problem from the cradle to the grave." If you have found the solution, with elimination of pollution, you are well on your way to resolution of your childhood inhibitions.

NOTE:
There was no utilization of the following words: condensation, explanation, capitulation, validation, distraction, ejection, ejaculation, diminution, rejection, assimilation, abrogation, sophistication, rumination, erection, election, elocution, evacuation, electrocution, optician, mortician, apprehension, tension, pretension, mediation, oxidation, peregrination, annulations, violation, hyphenation, exclamation, irrigation, memorization, ritualization, coeducation, molestation, germination, rotation, absorption, renegotiation, libation, recalibration, beautification, interrogation, infestation, imperfection, and classification.

P.S. The designation "Original Sin" was a promulgation of 7 elderly spinsters who were so ugly that couldn't get a husband. Simultaneously the phrase "sour grapes" came into being. Later, disciples of a Jewish man named Yossel did an incorporation of "Original Sin" into their own new religious revolution.

P.S.2. With great trepidation, I didn't list "perfection" because I knew there would be objection from most of you who have had notification from me that THERE IS NO PERFECTION!!

# Three Important Words

Here's an extra . . . more G.P. philosophy:

A few mornings ago I woke up feeling that something was going to be revealed to me. As I brushed my teeth, I heard a voice say, "Knowledge is great!" I then said to myself, "If knowledge is great, what is greater?" The answer came immediately: UNDERSTANDING.

I decided to take it further: "If understanding is greater, what is the greatest?" Again I got an immediate reply: FORGIVENESS.
Not too long ago I wrote that, in my opinion, forgiveness is the height of lovingness. And so we come right back to the old theme . . . the importance of love.

Then I thought of four people who had harmed me greatly. Two of them are dead. And I felt quite deeply that I could truly forgive them.

I hope this gives all of you food for thought. Review in your mind all those who harmed you or whom you despised for one reason or another. And then see if you can find it in your heart to forgive them.

MUCH LOVE -

Dad/GP

# *Three Little Words*

In the 1940s Harry Ruby and Bert Kalmer wrote that delightful tune, which catapulted into a movie in 1950, starring Fred Astaire and Red Skelton.

What does this information have to do with today's discussion? Virtually nothing! But it does offer me the opportunity to segue into my theme. There are "three little words" that I consider to be the most important words in the dictionary: REALITY, WONDERFUL, and LOVE.

Some time ago we talked a lot about LOVE, and last month was devoted to WONDERFUL. So, let's take a look at REALITY. What is the opposite of reality? Of course, it's fantasy. The human brain is so complex, with its conscious and unconscious divisions working overtime so often that many persons have great difficulty distinguishing between fantasy and reality.

A good friend of mine, Paul White, an excellent psychologist, told me that the common thread running through the psyches of virtually all his patients is "low self-esteem" which he says is a fantasy.

"A compensatory measure by these same patients," he added, "is the unconscious fantasy of omnipotence or perfection, which also is a fantasy."

It behooves all of us to look at ourselves, our relatives, our friends... even the world... with an honest perspective and, hopefully, live in reality.

Now, the word "wonderful" comes into play. As you ruminate, or just casually appraise things, give the word "wonderful" a big opportunity to color your views. You don't have to become a Pollyanna, which also is a fantasy, but think as positively and realistically as possible. You'll probably find that you are much more wonderful than you thought, and this concept of "wonderfulness" becomes quite positive.

This brings up the third word, LOVE, which is the most wonderful positive force in the universe. Use your love to cement your relationships with yourself and others. Loving deeply can be more heady than a glass of wine. Love can change me from an old curmudgeon to a blithe spirit. Love is the strong base for all religious thought and all our good deeds. Loving yourself is the greatest gift you can give yourself.

Summing up, please remember the three most important words: "REALITY, LOVE, and WONDERFUL." In reality, we all love one another, and that is quite wonderful!

MUCH LOVE....    ❑ Dad    ❑ G.P.

P.S. Copies of this month's issue are going to my sisters and a few close friends. In reality, they are all wonderful and I love them too.

P.P.S.    How coincidental!!  The song "Three Little Words" ends in its meaning, "I LOVE YOU!"

# *Three More Words*

We were very fortunate to have had a lovely visitor from Maine last month. She is well-versed in Buddhism, so I insisted that she talk on that subject at our Lighthouse support group meeting.

She was wonderful and the group appreciated her learned discussion. I liked it tremendously because I got THREE MORE WORDS to add to our list.

The first one is ACCEPTANCE. She spoke of accepting pain as a precursor to getting well. I thought of it as acceptance of all reality - one of our first three words. The person who accepts reality with a feeling of well-being is well-adjusted.

The next word is GRATEFULNESS. We have discussed this before in the context of "count your blessings - love yourself" for those with eye problems. Of course, this is important for everyone, and gratefulness is the first step toward equanimity.

The third word is FORGIVENESS. This word ties in beautifully with one of our first three words, love. I feel that forgiving those who harmed you is the height of lovingness. It also is extremely important to the forgiver, for the forgiver benefits even more than those forgiven. He, or she, is loving him- or herself.

When we accept reality, and we are grateful for all the good things we have, and we extend forgiveness to others, we are truly wonderful and living in love, instead of hate.

MUCH LOVE from the old preacher,

❏ Dad    ❏ G.P.

# The Buddha
# Is Inside You

On April 27th, 2002, my wife, son David and I went to the Osolo Theater to see a wonderful comedy, "The Allergist's Wife." During the play, the Allergist's wife, a ditzy liberal, was constantly referring to her great love, the book Siddartha by Herman Hesse.

At the end of the play, when the comedy turned to philosophy, one of the minor characters turned to the Allergist's wife and said, "The Buddha is inside you." This comment was like an electric shock to me, because my immediate translation of BUDDHA was LOVE!

In my missive, "Maxim-ize Your Life," I wrote a lot about love:

Love is the most grateful force in the world.

Live in love instead of hate.

I'm counting my blessings and loving myself–a mantra.

There are many different kinds of love–all of them good.

We must love each other or live in a constant state of antagonism. (Auden revised)

Forgiveness is the height of lovingness.

The modern sophisticated person has two major drives: food and sex. (I'm now changing "sex" to "love."

After reading the above comments, it's easy to see why I was so smitten with the line, "The Buddha is inside you." If I'm right in assuming that Buddha is love, then everything is clear. We all need love and approval, but if that love and approval is inside us, that is, if we truly love ourselves, we can be warm, loving, caring human beings. And this warmth and love will beget love and approval from our spouses, relatives, and friends.

Consciously or unconsciously, you are the only one who knows about your inner feelings. You alone know about the meanness, the pettiness, the covetous, the greediness, and your angriness. But now that you know the Buddha [love] is inside you, you can forgive yourself for your negative humanness and love yourself exactly as you are! This, in turn, permits you to love others exactly as they are.

Your Buddha can become a beacon of light, brightening you inside and helping you illuminate a dingy world.

Love that Buddha!

Love - Dad/Grandpa

# Plover

Plover is a bird, but it's also an acronym for Present . . . LOVE . . . and REALITY.

A few months ago I advised you to live in the present not the past, live in love not hate, and to live in reality not fantasy. Let me elaborate on that now.

In the past, our early childhood, everyone was so huge and a bit frightening as they programmed and brainwashed you (more on that later). In the present, you are fully grown and capable of making your own decisions, with accompanying responsibilities. Too many people live in the past and they suffer with childhood conflicts.

LOVE is the "biggie!" That's why it's spelled out. The opposite of love is hate, which is also anger and rage in various gradations. Talk yourself out of your anger, rage and hatred. Let your feelings out but then calm them down. Love has many meanings, but the two greatest are the love for your mate, and the love for yourself.

All of the above is reality, but the opposite of reality is fantasy. This is one way of handling your so-called "bad feelings" . . . it's called "denial." But—you're better off living in reality and handling your feelings, rather than denying them.

So I say to you: fly high like a PLOVER and you'll be in clover!

MUCH LOVE,

Dad/GP

# Interdependency

In one of my missives, I advised you to remember three words which I considered the most important: love, wonderful, and reality. Please add this fourth one: INTERDEPENDENCY.

When we are babies, we are completely dependent. WRONG. The baby is giving the parents love, which is the chief ingredient in an interdependent relationship.

Sometimes the ratio is 50/50, other times 60/40, up to 90/10. I have been in the latter and find it rewarding because the 10 is love.

In the book (and picture) "Tuesdays With Morrie," the dying professor quotes Auden who says, "We must love each other or perish." My interpretation of that quote is that the whole world lives in an interdependency and that the chief ingredient of life, LOVE, must be with us or we die.

Psychologists tell us that children who are unhappy retreat in fantasy to the womb where they felt they were completely independent. Of course, the opposite is true.

So, let's live in reality, with wonderful love as we live in interdependent relationships.

MUCH LOVE,
Dad, G.P.

P.S.

I thought I'd go back to the one page format, but I'm now a garrulous old man and I want to add some additional thoughts on interdependency.

One of the first messages was about Aristotle's "golden mean"...excess and deficit, as he put it. I call it the happy medium. Loren says "everything in moderation, even moderation."

This concept has great bearing on the dependency issue. Complete dependency is "excess" and complete independence is "defect." Interdependency is the "happy medium." To carry it into a different context, it's not "all or nothing at all" which is a syndrome some people fall into.

On page one, I spoke in generalities. Let me give you a specific example. I need Stan, Paul (the gardener), Mike (the pool man), Marlene (the cleaning lady), and Ann (the cook). They work for me and I pay them - interdependency. But most of all, I need love. So I love my wife, my dog, my children, and my grandchildren... and they love me in return. Ergo! Interdependency! I like loving and I'm so happy that we are a loving family.

# Oedipal Shmedipal

There's a wonderful old story about a Jewish lady who went to see her son's psychiatrist. When she asked him what was wrong with her son, he said, "He has a deep seated Oedipal Complex." She replied, "Oedipal shmedipal, as long as he loves his mother!"

Yes, dear friends, Freud was so right with his Oedipus complex theory. I have thought about it a lot and have to conclude that so much of the lives of all people revolve about their sexual feelings and their huge guilt about the origination of these feelings with the opposite parent.

For example, look at the usage of the F word on the screen and real life. Add to that: M.F...bastard, son-of-a-bitch, etc., etc.

I have also observed that sports, which until recently were all male, have strong sexual overtones. In basketball they go for "the hole." In hockey, the puck is shot into the aperture to the net, and then "sieve." In soccer, the ball must be shot into the hole created by the uprights and the cross bar, and in football, it is kicked over the top.

I'm not saying that all our neuroses emanate from our sexual problems and conflicts, but it's truly a good place to start.

So here's to Freud, a nice Jewish boy who really "scored."

MUCH LOVE-

❏ G.P.   ❏ Dad

# More Thoughts on Religion

When I heard Vicki read the article about the Passover service before we began, I realized immediately that I must write more about religion. The comments about the symbolism and metaphor of the service gave credence to my comments last month. But it dawned on me that I didn't dwell enough on the positive side of religion.

Yes, I firmly believe that man created God, and that much of the thinking of those creators was to help people to desire to be good instead of the negativism of the law. And, by making God a huge cop in the sky, they preyed on our conscience.

On the other hand, if man created God and religion, there must have been a real need for it. We have only to emanate the hundreds of religions and their importance to so many people.

There is innate goodness in almost everyone, and our spiritual selves are warmed by the good deed, sacrifices, and love of others. Our spiritual aspect can weep on hearing a good symphony, a dramatic play, or a wonderful story.

And, on the positive side of religion, I must note its importance at weddings, funerals, and other life cycle events.

My brief is with religionists who are so slighted that they feel theirs is the only religion and are willing to fight for it and do. I also take issue with the dogma that permits no individual thought. In most religions, I would be a heretic and atheist for my recent writings.

So, as our good friend Aristotle postulated: look for the Golden Mean. There is a happy medium.

And, as one religious skunk said to the other religious skunk… let us pray!!! Nuff said about religion except one thing. I think it should be more personal.

Thanks to all of you for making my 85th birthday the best one ever. As I wrote to somebody, I couldn't have done better if I planned it myself.

MUCH LOVE -
❏ Dad   ❏ G.P.

# Happiness

Today I am writing about two thoughts of wisdom that complement each other:

(1) HAPPINESS COMES FROM THE INSIDE

(2) THE HAPPY MAN IS HE WHO IS CONTENT WITH HIS LOT

If you add these thoughts to the two I tell my visually impaired people, you have a design for good mental health:

(1) COUNT YOUR BLESSINGS

(2) LOVE YOURSELF

The soap box is carefully put away, after I dismounted, and I can tell you that I am no paragon. I must constantly remind myself to heed the above admonitions. Try it! It can be helpful!

Love,

❑ Dad  ❑ G.P.

# *Happiness Revisited*

Last month I wrote, in part, about happiness, but I think it bears further exploration.

As I see it, everyone's concept of happiness is different. Charlie is happy if I give him a treat or if he snuggles in his mama's lap. Some people are unhappy living in the lap of luxury, while others in very meager circumstances are quite happy.

What is your happiness quotient? Is it winning at gambling or bridge, or rooting your favorite team to victory?

Let's all remember the two maxims I've quoted before: happiness comes from inside - and - the happy man is he who is content with his lot.

Then it is incumbent on us to discover what "lot" we can be happy with and how we can become happy inside.

MUCH LOVE
❏ G.P.  ❏ Dad

P.S. My happiness will be enhanced when I see all of you in Chicago!!

P.S.2 Don't forget - "Love is the key to happiness"

# Reality Revisited and Renewal Revisited

Last month I wrote about the importance of living in reality, not in fantasy. Upon further reflection, I realize now that is easier said than done. The trouble is that people live in fantasy, convinced that it is reality.

A horrible example is Adolph Hitler. I think that he believed his fantasies were true: that the Germans were a super race, that the Jews were truly despicable, and that he could rule the world. He almost made the latter true.

Then there are those who are certain that they are destined to save the world, when in reality, they cannot save themselves.

If there is confusion between reality and fantasy, I support counseling or therapy. This is the real work of therapists.

RE: RENEWAL REVISITED... I haven't the least idea what I meant by that, but it made a great headline!!

MUCH LOVE -

❏ Dad    ❏ G.P.

# Renewal Revisited

I fooled you . . . but I also fooled myself when I saw the opportunity to renew our vows to (1) count our blessings and (2) love myself. And to revisit some of the salient factors in those two vows.

When I visited Ellis Island in July, I was quite emotional because this is where my grandparents entered the US. What a blessing to count: that we are citizens of this great country only because your grandparents and great-grandparents had the courage to leave family and friends to start a new life in a country with a language they didn't know and with virtually no money. How many of you know that Grandpa [Zadye] and Grandma Hechtman walked from Odessa to Hamburg, where they boarded a ship for the US? It took them weeks .

And the things we take for granted : plenty of good food, educational opportunities, sufficient money, great hospitals and doctors. These are advantages that most of the inhabitants of the world don't have.

Go ahead and dig. You'll find blessings galore. Think about them on the days you are blue and feeling sorry for yourself.

LOVING YOURSELF is not easy. It requires effort and practice. This is because you are your strongest critic. Many of us have a tendency to criticize and deprecate ourselves because we don't meet the standards we have set.

A good exercise is to think of all the people who admire you and love you. If they can do it, why not you? I fall into the latter category: I love and approve of all of you very much.

GP/Dad

# Metaphysics & Metapsychological

The first word, metaphysics, was defined for me (when I was in college 65 years ago) as "what is ultimately real." Since I am a complete and successful non-scientist, I have accepted that definition.

Actually, it has helped me to conceptualize the other word, metapsychological, a word which I minted. You will not find it in any dictionary or in any other lexicon but my own. And now, dear ones, I am passing it on to you.

My reasoning is that if metaphysics is "what is ultimately real," my new word means "what is ultimately important."

Since I can only afford one page at a time, I'll leave you to ruminate about this word and the various ramifications of the definition.

Of course, I'll expound on it subsequently, so... you can wait for those words of wisdom with bated breath.

MUCH LOVE -

❏ Dad  ❏ G.P.

# Unbate Your Breath

Unbate your breath, and listen to the wisdom of the ages... I mean aged. I'm certain you're all anxious to learn about the new PSYCHOLOGICS.

First of all, let's examine Charlie, or Cuzco, or Epiney, or Daisy, or Eddie. They fall into the category of "animals." But - we humans do too. My good friend and son, Howard, tells me that in the Buddhist thirty-two levels of being, man has only reached the fifth level.

Now, all the above mentioned dogs have two great needs, or, putting it in the context of our study, what is ultimately important to them is FOOD and LOVE.

Thus, these two major needs are ours also. To expand the FOOD section, it includes shelter, clothing, etc. And LOVE too has many ramifications.

Now, this brings me to the question of what is ultimately important and I say YOU and LOVE. You are your best friend or, at least, you should be. You should not only love yourself, but you should make every effort to make your life comfortable and productive. Be proud of yourself and your achievements. It takes the work of a lot of people in our interdependent society with all its complexities to permit us to live in peace and harmony.

Now we come to the most important ingredient in our lives: LOVE!! Without it, we could fall from the fifth place on the Buddhist ladder, and with it, we can probably climb higher.

There are so many types of love. Of course, after your love of yourself is the love of your mate. Nothing in life can be more gratifying than the love of your mate, and his or her love for you. But then, you love your dog and/or cat, your wonderful relatives, and mankind in general. Some people are hard to love but, in reality, they need it the most.

Going on... there's love of learning, love of nature, love of art, love of beauty, love of music... the list is endless.

Note: I didn't say love of money, because that is, according to some philosopher, the root of all evil. Money is important only for what it can buy, and a certain amount is necessary. Always remember, you can't buy money with happiness (or something like that.)

I am truly proud of all my children and grandchildren whose great interests lie in the non-material things in life and their interest and love of their fellow man. I write this message in love, and send to all of you all my love.

❏ Dad    ❏ G.P.

# Savor the Flavor

Savor the flavor of a cool breeze as you take your morning walk. And savor the flavor of the beautiful trees, shrubs, and flowers on the way. Then come home to breakfast and savor the flavor of the hot oatmeal with its succulent raisins, plumped by the heat and the ripe banana that has been virtually melted into the oatmeal. Then savor the flavor of the fresh coffee.

There is so much to savor... the kiss from your beloved that sometimes tingles your toes and the subsequent joining in a fantastic loving experience...is a good example.

You can savor a trip... perhaps a cruise to Alaska with one's dear family, and perhaps that flavor might linger for years. Or you can savor the flavor of a trip to, say, New Haven to see a grandchild get a degree. And you can savor the flavor of the camaraderie with the loved ones who have joined you at the ceremony.

There is so much more to savor: The warmth of your dog as he lays next to you, the softness of your cat's fur as you pet her.

Then there is the flavor to savor of a good play, a ballet, a symphony so beautiful that it brings tears to your eyes, or an opera with its stirring arias and beautiful music.

Savor the flavor of winning, whether it is at bridge, Mah Jong, tennis, or even watching your favorite team as it is successful.

Savor the flavor of a good night's sleep or the relaxation of exercise, meditation, or yoga.

You can savor the flavor of meaningful friendships with their emails, phone calls, and visits.

If you can savor many or all of these flavors, you're to be congratulated, because you are a warm, loving person savoring the many flavors of LIFE.

The French have a lovely phrase that seems to be savoring life as you say it slowly: La Joie de Vivre... the joy of life. And the ancient Hebrews toasted with an unforgettable phrase which I leave with you: L'chaim - to life!

MUCH LOVE-

GP - Dad

SAVOR IT!!

# Fasting

This month's message is about FASTING!

I woke up Yom Kippur morning and felt good. So I decided to fast. Not only did the fast go well, but I found it exhilarating. The ancient Hebrews were pretty smart! They knew that fasting makes you count your blessings and love yourself.

MUCH LOVE, Dad/GP

# Philosophy of the Psyche

FROM: Gershom Cohn

TO: All his children and grandchildren

RE: PHILOSOPHY OF THE PSYCHE

We come into the world screaming and kicking because we have been evacuated from the security and warmth and complete dependency of the womb.

And we leave this earth screaming and kicking because we want to live forever and we are afraid of death.

In between these two events, we go about screaming and kicking because we don't have everything exactly as we would like them to be.

If all the above sounds depressing, don't worry about it. Just remember the Golden Rule, the happy medium, and you'll make it with flying colors.

And remember the maxim that was on the wall of my father's office:

NOTHING THAT HAPPENS TO YOU IS AS BAD AS YOU THINK - NOR IS IT AS GOOD AS YOU THINK.

# Two Mantras

I have been helped greatly by the repetition of two mantras. The first one is:

IT'S SO GREAT TO BE ALIVE!

Ever since Ruth died so suddenly, and the death of three Bridge players at our club, I have been consumed by thoughts of death. And, of course, my own was paramount. The mantra, though, has convinced me that in the eons of time, we all have very short lives. This also convinced me that life is for the living and that we should enjoy our lives to the utmost. Every day is valuable.

The second mantra is more complicated. It is:

IT'S REALLY GREAT TO BE A MELLOW FELLOW!

I coined the term "Mellow Fellow" a few years ago and I have worked hard to be one inside and out. I think I can now be a "Mellow Fellow."

First of all, a Mellow Fellow aspires to have peace and tranquility, equanimity and compassion, joy and happiness. Most importantly, he does what the psychologists call "holding the opposites." Here are a number of them:

LOVE - HATE: I was surprised to find that love and hate can exist in the body at the same time. It's a job to hold them both, but WE DO HAVE CHOICE!

PERFECTION - WORTHLESSNESS: There is no perfection nor is there worthlessness. This is probably the greatest feeling problem. But, there is a lot of WORTHWHILE in all of us and all of life.

REACHING OUT - WITHDRAWAL: Here we have the famous "withdrawal in the womb"
in which the very young child wishes to return from where he came be-

cause he (or she) can't cope with the vicissitudes of life. It's a bad choice and sometimes continues through life in fantasy. Holding the opposites here helps maintain proper balance.

ACCEPTANCE - REJECTION: This is quite similar to withdrawal and reaching out, but it's more extreme. I have told you many times that "acceptance" is the key to happiness. Conversely, rejection, whether overt or covert, can hurt you. There are times you deem it best to do one or the other. You have choice!

HETEROSEXUALITY - HOMOSEXUALITY: It is a known fact that both feelings exist in everyone to varying degrees. Again - it's your choice!

DEPENDENCY - INDEPENDENCY: Hold these both and opt for the happy medium. Interdependency is wonderful!

FANTASY - REALITY: Some people live all of their lives in fantasy. I suppose a little fantasy takes the sharp edges off the unvarnished truth. Hold them both and let your inner self tell you what is best for you.

LIFE - DEATH: When I wrote about Ruth's death, I said I was consumed by death. I think everyone thinks about death when they get older. Hold them both and live each day with enjoyment.

FEAR - COURAGE: Another opposite that has been with you all of your life. In holding them both, you can eliminate your fears and have the courage to succeed.

WINNING - LOSING: Everyone wants to win, but there are others who are afraid to win. These are truly opposites and must be held tightly if you want to conquer your fears.

INNOCENCE - GUILT: Societal pressure and pressure from misguided parents have made us feel guilty of almost all our feelings. A good example is one of the Ten Commandments, which we hold so dearly. It is "THOU SHALT NOT COVET." There we are made guilty of a feeling we cannot stop. Everyone covets. The problem comes when we turn the feeling into action. I'm convinced that guilt and shame makes people buy a lot of aspirin and sleeping pills. Hold them both and realize that you are completely innocent if they are only feelings.

MISERY - HAPPINESS: We tend to vacillate from one to the other. Even things out by holding both.

I think you can see why it took so long for me to be a "Mellow Fellow." Why not join me?!!!

MUCH LOVE,

❑ Dad  ❑ Grandpa  ❑ Gersh

# To Live is to Suffer

I was surprised to hear these philosophical words from a noted politician on television, as he used them to make a point about those who suffer from lack of health care.

I know about it a lot, and it came into my mind repeatedly, because there is great truth there. People have physical pain for numerous reasons and then there is the mental and emotional pain from stress, anxiety, conflict, guilt, and shame that has been passed on by parents and society.

But - before you rush out to buy a gun to put an end to your suffering - I have good news for you. There is the opposite side that says: "Life is joy and happiness." I think it's safe to say that this is the positive that we should emphasize.

A small example: Ruth comes over and I give her a big hug. She tells me that she had been feeling depressed and now feels good. The same for me! So, I recommend hugging a loved one to turn your feelings to the positive side of life. Or else have your grandchildren and great-grandchildren come to visit you! It's a real "upper!"

All of this is an example of "emphasizing the opposite" which I promised to write about. A good friend of mine theorizes that everything has an opposite. How true!

In my old age, I'm indulging in giving out advice and acting like a wise old seer. Thus, I'll tell you that you're going to suffer in varying degrees as you go through life, but you can also live in joy and happiness if you keep in mind a phrase that was given to me when my wife died:

LIFE IS GOOD - I CHOOSE TO BE HAPPY!!

# Joy & Happiness

My daughter, Arlene, says I'm getting to be a sage... in my old age. Here are some more thoughts that can be helpful:

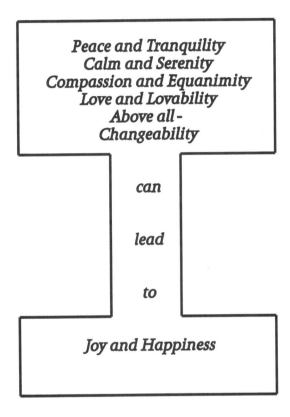

*Peace and Tranquility*
*Calm and Serenity*
*Compassion and Equanimity*
*Love and Lovability*
*Above all -*
*Changeability*

*can*

*lead*

*to*

*Joy and Happiness*

At first blush, these words may sound a little platitudinous. However, as you repeat these words they tend to negate the tensions and conflicts that everyone possesses.

More importantly, they form a base for the self-confidence that is so necessary to solve our problems and to understand ourselves and our fellow man.

Note that the diagram above is in the form of an "I." This coincides with the advice that the leader of our bereavement group gave us. At the first meeting, the first thing she said was "You are all senior citizens who have lost your mates. Now is the time to be selfish. Coddle yourself. Be kind to yourself and love yourself. For now, you are #1!"

# I Choose to be Happy

When I was in the depths of my despondency over the loss of my wife, Pitzel, (my niece Peggy) insisted that I talk to Kali Das, who heals people with nutrition and kinetics. I don't really recall what we talked about, but I do remember well the two maxims that he gave me: LIFE IS GOOD AND I CHOOSE TO BE HAPPY. They are both quite powerful for many reasons.

As many of you know, I love to quote Thoreau, who said, "The masses lead lives of quiet desperation." I have modified it to: "Most people lead lives of quiet desperation."

Thoreau was probably referring to those who live in poverty, as the masses do. But I feel that the majority of people, with their external and internal pains have negative outlooks on life. An easy example is the billions of over-the-counter pills that are sold every year such as aspirin, other pills for pain, and pills for sleep. Not to mention the tons of alcohol and drugs... all designed to ease the pain.

So - why are the two maxims I'm discussing so powerful? It's because they are so positive! LIFE IS GOOD is the exact opposite of those who are depressed and feel helpless and hopeless. Many commit suicide, while others contemplate it. That, of course, is the extreme. But millions do take a negative view toward life. Just repeating LIFE IS GOOD can raise your spirits.

I CHOOSE TO BE HAPPY says "You have choice." You can get a hold of your negative emotions and live a happier and more productive life. Inherent in this positive statement is a gentle put-down of all your negativism. Remember, it is easier to be negative than positive.

We all have our low moments, because we are human beings. My suggestion is that when you do have troubles and feel miserable, try repeating "Life is good. I choose to be happy" as a mantra. And, when it works, you can say "Thank you, Kali Das."          MUCH LOVE,
❏ Dad,   ❏ GP,   ❏ Cousin   ❏ Friend

# Gratefulness

My cousin Ruthmary Cohn sent me a list of everything she does at breakfast time. It was quite lengthy. One item in her regimen intrigued me: her "grateful" box - in which she put all she was grateful for the previous day.

I have thought about that a lot and have come to conclude that most people are not grateful enough for all the good things that happen in their lives.

Here's a quick example. I was walking with Charlie this morning when two trucks passed us. I noted the noxious fumes and thought about the impact of thousands of cars as they drive bumper-to-bumper in our cities. But - I wasn't grateful for the pure air I inhaled after the trucks had gone. I just took it for granted.

The ancient Hebrews had great wisdom. They devised prayers thanking God for everything that happens to them. They're always grateful for their sexual activity and even a good B.M.

I don't have to delineate here all the things we should be grateful for. But I must tell you that this extremely positive attitude will make you a happier person.

At this point in my life, with the recent events at the hospital, I am extremely grateful to the doctors and nurses, who have prolonged my life. I'm grateful for my capable brain and my body which is now getting stronger. Most of all, I'm grateful for my wonderful family which rallied around me in my latest crisis; and for the love they gave to me.

Think about it! Write down your gratefulness. I promise… you'll be well rewarded!

MUCH LOVE,

❏ Dad,   ❏ GP,   ❏ GGP

# *Acceptance*

"For all the words of tongue and pen; the saddest are it might have been."

I don't know who wrote that... sounds like Shakespeare or Bobby Burns... but I do know they summarize a great concept. And that is to accept things as they are, or were, unless you plan to make the effort to change them.

A good example is duplicate bridge. Some say the name should be changed to: "woulda, coulda, shoulda," because players are inclined to be so recriminatory. In reality, the game is over and we have to accept all the consequences. It's true that you can work to correct the mistakes you have made, but that is constructive as well as accepting.

My good friend Ruth says "and that's the way it is." Reminds me of Walter Cronkite who ended his program with "and that's the way it was." Both are "accepting."

If you can accept things as they are, you will relieve yourself of the burden of being perfect. My best mantra regarding acceptance is "All is well, so what the hell." Think about that - there's a lot a lot of acceptance in the phrase, and it's quite succinct.

As I write about acceptance, it suddenly occurs to me that acceptance is the key to happiness. It embodies all the positive feelings of friendliness, compassion, kindness, and yes, love. And - just as charity begins at home - so does acceptance.

If we can accept ourselves with all our weaknesses, foibles, strengths and humanness, we're well on the road to happiness.

I love all of you exactly as you are and I want you to reciprocate.

MUCH LOVE -

Dad/G.P.

# *Death!!*

In discussing death with Vicki a few years ago, she came up with this very interesting observation, "Man is the only animal who knows he is going to die." This gave me a lot of food for thought, as I set about inquiring into my own thoughts and feelings about death.

David told me recently that he uses the word "death" as a mantra. He said that constant repetition of the word seems to bring him peace and relaxation. I tried it and found that he is right. Please do so before you read the rest of this piece.

Seven or eight years ago I was in "Group Therapy" with four other men past 70. We discussed death a number of times, and I have talked about death with other senior citizens. The consensus was that (1) no one wanted to die, (2) the thought was anathema to many, (3) all agreed on it's inevitability, (4) most felt that it was the end ... no afterlife (5) many were afraid of death, and (6) death is a part of life.

It is only natural that as we become older, we think about death. We write wills, and do all sorts of planning for our demise. This is the realistic and practical preparation for death.

But, what is there about the word that makes it such a powerful mantra? I can think of two reasons. Firstly, in our unconscious as well as our conscious minds, there is a fear of death. Somehow, the constant repetition of the word lessens that fear and helps us come to grips with its inevitability and our powerlessness to stop it. I think it brings better acceptance.

Secondly, the constant repetition becomes peaceful, and we can contemplate the peacefulness of dying. Some people either "pull the plug" or stop eating because they really want to die.

My third reason may cause some raised eyebrows, but I truly believe that there is in everyone a fear of their own capacity to commit murder, and that this fear is assuaged by the mantra.

Psychiatrists have come up with the phrase "the death wish." This is a step by step process from anger to rage to hatred to the "death wish." How many people have said, "I was so mad at him (or her) I could have killed him." Recently, my friend Lee Weinberger said facetiously, "Carl better not die... if he does I'll kill him!"

You see, it is a feeling, not an act, but it is not a feeling we are proud of. In fact, most everyone denies the "death wish" feelings that are really quite normal. But the constant repetition of the word "death" can ease the fear we have that we might commit such an atrocious act.

So I leave you with the fond hope that you can come to grips with death and come to realize that it can be a beautiful ending to a life well lived. David tells me that his hospice friends have a relaxed and positive view about their death.

A few years ago I wrote about "Le Chaim," the Jewish toast to life. Today I say, "to death!: May you all live a long and happy life, and come to grips with your conflicts about what can be a joyous and peaceful event.

# Life

Last month I wrote about "death," so I think it is appropriate to write about "life" now. As they do in the movies, this becomes a "flashback," because "life" does precede "death."

Before I give you my views on "life," I want to relate some thoughts that I left out last month. I spoke of "death" as a mantra and then wrote a lot about "death wish." For me, the "death wish" is a superior mantra. Perhaps that is because I left out the other side of the coin... the "death wish" for you!

Yes, there are many people who unconsciously or perhaps consciously, hate themselves. They know all the "horrible" thoughts and desires they have and they hate themselves. Thus, they conclude that this horrible person should be eliminated. Think of the problem we have now... teenage suicide... and all the people who have killed others and then themselves.

Then there is the painting that hangs in our foyer. It was created by Professor Jordan, the head of the art department at Washington University. It was hung in the office of the President, but it was for sale. David wanted it for his graduation and he got it. When he went west, he gave it to us for safe-keeping. We are doing just that... and he gets it back when we die.

Please look at it carefully when you visit us. It is called "a time to die" and it is a scrawny old man with a flowing beard, and he is simply fading away. The colors are beautiful and so is the concept. It truly depicts what I wrote last month about dying with dignity and release from all earthly cares and woes.

Enough about "death." Let's talk about life. What does the word connote to you? Replace the "E" with the letter "T" and it will give you a "lift." The word itself has vigor and enthusiasm. Example: "She's full of life."

The French have a beautiful phrase about life: LA JOIE DE VIVRE...the joy of life. Just repeating it sounds joyful.

And so it is... a real joy to be alive. We fight for it all our lives, with good nutrition, proper medication, and operations when necessary. It is so important to stay alive. Vicki tells me that her best mantra is following her breathing. And that tells me that this exercise is telling me to calm down, not to worry, we're breathing and still alive. All is well.

The ancient Hebrews knew well what they were doing when they decreed that Yom Kippur would be a day of fasting. After 24 hours of abstinence, the taste of water and food is fantastic. Life is wonderful!

The struggle for life goes on with criminals who have committed single or mass murder. They insist that their lawyers fight to the last gasp in the courtroom to save them from the electric chair. They'd rather spend the rest of their lives in jail.

What is the good life? What should we aspire to? How can we achieve it? My answer is to refer you to an old saying "there are many roads that lead to New York." In other words, each person must decide for himself what kind of life he should lead. We may not approve of all of them, but it's their lifestyle.

For some, it could be "wine, women, and song" or a gay life catering to our senses. Not bad... especially in moderation. Then there is the other extreme... a life of celibacy, such as nuns and priests, in which they live to serve others and spend their lives reading and studying.

For me, the good life lies in the middle. I like wine, woman, and song. And I also like doing things for others. I know that I have helped many people in my lifetime, personally and financially. I'm happy that I have been able to do so and I don't want any medals. The satisfaction one gets from his or her good deeds it its own reward. Some say that "no good deed goes unpunished" but I don't believe that.

Socrates said, "The unexamined life is not worth living." If that is true, I am greatly blessed! But I want to paraphrase that pithy thought to THE UNGENEROUS LIFE IS NOT WORTH LIVING.

I really feel sorry for the people who are not generous. Their attitude is epitomized by this true story. I asked a wealthy man for a contribution to UJA. This was in Decatur. I'll never forget his words, "Gersh, it hurts me to give." Yes, dear family, there are millions of people who are so selfish that it hurts them to give. Isn't that sad!

Perhaps the person who truly gives of himself (or herself) is the most selfish of all. The satisfaction they derive is far greater than that of one who figuratively lines his coffin with money.

I take great pride in all my children, grandchildren, and additions to our family for the way they all share their lives with others. Keep up the good work: be generous, be generous, and be generous. It is a way of life and for me it's the only way to live.

Generosity is just one aspect of a loving person. Others are kindness, compassion, understanding, and forgiveness. And they are all propelled by what I call the most powerful force in the world... LOVE!

P.S. Speaking of living and dying, as I have the last two months, I must admit that even though I want to experience the joy of death, I'd be most happy if that event would be postponed indefinitely!

# Oh Me Oh My

*Oh me oh my*
*I wonder why*
*We laugh and cry*
*and live and die*
*I sigh and sigh*
*for I must die*
*I do not lie*
*to say goodbye*
*I do decry*

OH ME OH MY
I WONDER WHY
WE LAUGH AND CRY
AND LIVE AND DIE
I SIGH AND SIGH
FOR ~~XXXX~~ I MUST DIE
I DO NOT LIE
TO SAY GOODBYE
~~~~O DECRY

# The Four Aspects of Man

It is my firm conviction that there are four aspects of man: physical, mental, emotional, and spiritual. I'm not a doctor, professor, psychologist, Rabbi, or neurologist, so I know that I'm being presumptuous in writing about this subject.

But–since I have a captive audience that is obliged to say how wonderfully I write, I'm going to do it.

This month's issue is an introduction to these earth shattering revelations. The next four months will be devoted to each of the aspects, and the last one will be my conclusion.

Actually, I intend to show that mankind has developed the physical and mental aspects, while neglecting the emotional and spiritual development.

MUCH LOVE - Dad/Grandpa

# The Physical and Mental Aspects of Man

I am writing about these two aspects together because they are so intertwined. In viewing the tremendous advances man has made physically, we note that advanced mental capacity has made them possible.

I read recently that my grandchildren will, in all likelihood, live to be one hundred years old or more. Advancements in medical science and nutrition are the major reasons. Grandma and I went to Protilair many years ago, and I see that many (or most) of the things he espoused are now common rules for good nutrition. My father died after three heart attacks because they knew so little about the problem of cholesterol. Yet, twenty-five years later, I was saved by a four-way bypass. And science has devised many other ways to extend life for heart patients.

Our support group was addressed by an ophthalmologist who told us that there will be an explosion in techniques to help people with eye problems in the next twenty years. We already have two methods that could have saved my sight if they were available fifteen years ago.

And there are tremendous advancements in cancer research, diabetes, virtually all of man's diseases.

There is so much to talk about as we see tremendous advancements in creature comforts: transportation, communication, entertainment... even our appliances.

When I was a baby my parents travelled by horse and buggy. We had railroads, of course, but then came the automobile, airplane, and perhaps we'll have interplanetary travel someday.

Not too long ago, communication was by pony express. Then came the telegraph, telephone, and postal mail. Now we have Fed-Ex and E-mail.

When I was little, my mother cooked on a coal range. I know about all those appliances because I sold them. Yes, I sold coal ranges, oil ranges, gas stoves, and electric ranges. I sold wood stoves, black round coal heaters and fancy coal heaters (Estate Heatrola).

I also sold iceboxes and wringer-type washing machines as well as the new modern versions which have become better and better.

Also in my lifetime, we went from player piano to phonograph, to radio, to television to computer pictures.

I could go on and on, but I'm certain that you get the picture. Man's increased mental capacity has developed advancements in every phase of our life and activity.

Plus the tremendous advances in education and information. They call this the INFO-MATION ERA. The internet and computers are spewing out information in huge quantities, and our schools and libraries are loaded with more and more books.

As you can see, this is not a scholarly paper - going way back in time - but merely my own observances of the tremendous strides that have been taken in our physical and mental aspects.

I might add that writing two pages at one time with my C.C.T.V. has exhausted me!!

MUCH LOVE

❑ Dad    ❑ G.P.

# The Emotional Aspect of Man (or Woman)

We have observed that man is an animal and (as such) has two main drives: FOOD & PROPAGATION. We also noted that man is an phenomenon in nature: he has an active brain and uses it tremendously and he is quite complex.

This brings us to his emotionalism which is very limited in other animals. Man (and women) love deeply which usually leads to sexual expression. They also have feelings of anger, rage, hatred, fear, anxiety, guilt, and shame. There are also feelings of withdrawal and rejection.

When we looked at the religious aspect of man, we observed that the main objective of religion is to make man desire to be good, rather than to "stay in line" because of the punishment meted out by the establishment.

Unfortunately, the religionists went too far! They made people feel guilty because of their feelings. Thus, because of parental and societal pressure, children are taught to repress their feelings, rather than suppress them, which is the desired goal.

An extreme example is the Catholic Church, where the nuns, priests, bishops, cardinals, and the pope are celibate (supposedly). Jesus was born to a virgin mother. What does this do to a child when he feels natural sexual urges or how much damage is done to a child when he expresses his hatred verbally and a kindly but misguided parent says, 'you mustn't hate anyone."

So, all the repression can explode into rape, fondling of little children, arson, stealing, and murder. Timothy McVeigh worked for 3 years to prepare for his dastardly deed in Oklahoma City, and he expresses no real remorse for killing so many people.

His is an extreme example ... but there are millions of millions of neurotic people who live in pain all their lives with headaches, stomach pains and all kinds of psychosomatic disorders. Highly neurotic persons eat, drink, gamble, smoke, fornicate, and use drugs <u>excessively</u>. Others, in acting out the animal instinct to "fight or flee" withdraw to the womb (in fantasy, of course) and live in tension and conflict all their lives.

Now, let's take a look at psychiatry and psychology. It is comparatively new ... about 150 years ... and lacks credence with most people. Medical doctors give it short shrift. To them, there are no psychosomatic disorders. The average person says, "I don't need a therapist. I'm not crazy." Most Jewish Family Service organizations are placed in inconspicuous locations. This is done to protect the confidentiality of their clients who are ashamed to seek counseling.

Most psychiatrists now prescribe drugs for depression. I have to assume they have given up looking for deep-rooted causes (which is a long hard process) and settle for palliative measures.

I have said this many times and will say it again: everyone is neurotic; it's just a matter of degree.

So, what's the answer? Wait with bated breath for the July 1st edition, when Dr. G. R. Cohn will prescribe for the future

MUCH LOVE,

❏ G.P.   ❏ Dad

P.S. This didn't turn out as well as I wanted. So, I will talk to any or all of you about any of all of this.

# More on our Feelings

I felt that I erred when I omitted discussing Sigmund Freud last month when I wrote about the EMOTIONAL ASPECT OF MAN. After all, Freud is the father of psychiatry. How can I write about our neuroses without discussing Freud? So I dashed off the enclosed piece.

In re-reading it, I realized that I didn't make it clear that everyone is not infected with the oedipal virus. The normal progression is to grow up, get a love object of your own, and not feel guilty about your sexual feelings. This is the desired goal... along with being comfortable with all your feelings.

But, more about this in the August edition. I sincerely hope your bated breath will hold out another thirty days.

Your mother... G.M.... and I are enjoying the nice, warm sunshine here in Sarasota. We're now into 90°+ weather and the pool is a welcome relief.

MUCH LOVE

❏ Dad   ❏ G.P.

# The Spiritual Aspect of Man

Man, or should I say humankind, is a phenomenon in nature. He thinks... and he thinks a lot about how to handle his normal animal instincts. And there is a spiritual quality about mankind that cannot be denied.

Before I inveigh about formal religion and its repetitive practices, I want to go on record as a deeply religious person who believes that the basic tenets of all religions (love of yourself and others, generosity, and goodness) are wonderful.

Now, let's go back to the ancient Greeks and Romans with their myriad of gods and goddesses. Then came the Hebrews with their concept of one God and their promulgation of "love thy neighbor as thyself." This concept has been incorporated in virtually every religion.

They also gave us the Ten Commandments, which, by their negative portions... THOU SHALT NOT... are in direct contrast with man's animal nature. Animals will kill for food, animals will kill their rivals for sex, animals will steal... and all without conscience.

I firmly believe that man created God, not God created man. And I also believe that the leaders, in their wisdom, were trying to create an instrument (with religion) to control man's behavior by making him will to be good - the positive way - and by creating a conscience to further keep him in line.

When the Romans adopted Christianity, they chose it over Judaism because it was much simpler. But they did this to keep the masses mollified, and to give them some hope for a better life in the hereafter. Remember the quote from Thoreau, "The masses live lives of quiet desperation."

I don't dislike formal religion. I enjoy the wedding ceremony and our high holidays. Funerals, too, are important. I even found the Catholic mass fascinating.

My quarrel with religion is its repetitiveness... its rites, rituals, and dogma... its sameness. The Orthodox Jewish service is the same as it was thousands of years ago. And the same goes for Catholic and Christian services.

Too much emphasis is placed on repetitive practices and not enough time spent on the important facets of our religious life.

And the fighting! Millions have been killed because of differences over religious concepts. It's going on today with diverse units of Moslems and Hindus.

All of the above has been sort of a rambling of my thoughts on religion and spirituality. But I am leading up to my conclusion that little progress has been made in the past 2000 years. We must believe because the Bible (or Koran) says it. We must follow tradition.

In my opinion, religion must be more progressive. It must respond to the many changes in our society by helping more people with their spiritual needs. We don't drive around in a horse and buggy or cook on a coal range. Why, then, do we practice our religion the same way as we did in day 1, year 1?

Too many religious leaders are in conflict with our psychiatrists and psychologists and vice versa. Yet, the real need is for them to work together to calm the demons inside. More on this in the next issue.

As I did some time ago, I'll paraphrase Thoreau, "Most people lead lives of quiet desperation." If this is true, it is a problem for our religionists, psychologists, and psychiatrists to work on. AMEN & AMEN!

MUCH LOVE,
___ G.P.   ___ Dad

P.S. BMs AND METAPHORS

This piece was scheduled for May but it is such a vital part of our spiritual aspects that I'm including it now.

Everyone knows what BMs are. They are BUBBAMICAS, which is literally "stories" of my grandmother... or wonderful stories with slight (or complete) embellishment.

Let's go back thousands of years to when the Jews were nomads or lived in small villages. And here comes the travelling storyteller with news of other settlements and wonderful "micas."

I can hear the people yelling at the storyteller, "Tell us the one about Jonah and the whale," and then he would regale them with wonderful tales about Noah and the Ark, Abraham and Isaac, Esther and Haman, Joseph and his brothers, Moses and the Ten Commandments, etc., etc.

Ultimately, these BMs became the written words and they filled up the Torah and the Old Testament. As stories go, when they were passed on zillions of times, the final version is quite different from the original.

The biggest BM of all times is the story about Jesus. The New Testament was written one hundred years after Jesus lived. Jesus and his friends (later called disciples) were young liberal Jews who objected to bad practices such as "money changing" in the Temple. This might have been gambling. They wanted to reform Judaism, not found a new religion.

But one hundred years later, the BM is about his "virgin" birth and his death on the cross and how he died for our sins.

Hey! That's a lot of BM. Yet, it is believed literally by academicians, leaders of our country, our largest corporations, and the world of science. In the BM naming Jews as the ones who killed Christ, the inference was that all Jews were terrible people who should be punished. OY VEH! Have we been punished?

But now comes the good news: the metaphor. All the BMs had great meaning. They told of the triumph of good over evil, the inherent goodness of man, and pleaded with him to suppress his negative qualities and emphasize the positive ones.

So here comes the biggie: LOVE! This is truly the message of all religions. It's sad that we haven't learned our catechism of love well enough.

P.S. 2   To prove my point, I'd like you to get a video of "Cabin in the Sky." This is an old musical with an all-black cast that is quite wonderful.

It is an oversimplification of an oversimplification as it chronicles God's problems with the people on Earth.   E.G.   The last scene shows God stomping around saying sharply, "I have too much to do to handle those people down there." And then someone hands him a little bundle which he holds tenderly in his hands.   It's little baby Jesus!   Fade out... with a beautiful Negro spiritual.

# Conclusions

For the past several months we have been looking at the physical, mental, emotional, and spiritual aspects of man. Now it is time to end these observations with some conclusions. This will be in two parts: physical and mental as well as the emotional and spiritual. Not only do these four components fit well with this alignment, but the progress of each duality is markedly the same.

Yes, mankind has made tremendous strides in improving our physical and mental capacities. Modern medicine, in the past 50 years, has brought about tremendous breakthroughs in ophthalmology, heart disease, cancer, diabetes; in fact, every known disease has been attacked successfully. Although we don't follow the advice of our experts enough, we have plans laid out for us for exercise and nutrition that are truly life enhancing. In sports, for example, records are constantly being broken which is indicative of the improvement of our bodies. Another indicator is our longevity. I was told by a professor at New College that my grandchildren have a life expectancy of 100 years.

Our mental progress has worked hand-in-hand with our physical aspect, by providing all of the above benefits with research and development. Additionally, this is a whole new age - the information age - which is providing us with more knowledge than we can digest, and with this greater knowledge, we have developed health care programs that are still evolving. Advancements have been made also on the economic front with Social Security and a great effort to eliminate the old boom and bust with its debilitating depressions.

Of course, there are many other facets of our physical and mental aspects, to prove my point that there have been exceptional improvements in both these areas.

On the other hand, little progress has been made in our emotional and spiritual lives.

Let's start with the spiritual and the basic assumption I have made that man created God, not vise-versa. In truth, this is good because we need a God. It is not surprising that the word "good" is similar to "God" in thirteen languages. Man wants guidelines so that they can be good from a positive sense, rather than the negative of punishment by the state if he errs. Religion is a conservation of values such as truth, honesty, love, goodness, kindness, charity, and justice. We need the religiosity of a wedding, a funeral, the birth of a child, etc., etc.

But the religionists have become carried away with their own dogma. They believe all the beautiful fairy tales which metaphorically teach us great truths and dogmatically insist that their followers believe as they do and repeat (ad nauseam) paeans of praise to their deity. No attempt is made to change, modify, or improve their individual faith.

Moreover, they have gone too far with their guilt and shame (our conscience) which is hopefully designed to eliminate, or diminish, rape, murder, theft, incest, etc. Yes, they have gone too far by demanding that we deny our own feelings, which is impossible.

This brings us to our emotional aspect of man. It is the responsibility of every individual to handle his or her feelings. Too many times we see terrible outbreaks of crimes as an explosive device triggered by years of repression.

Psychiatry and psychology are truly the "new kids on the block" as their practitioners attempt to swell the tides of depression, conflict, tension, and fear that are the end result of the perfectionist goals that have been propounded in past generations and passed on from parent to child. There has been some progress in these areas but not nearly enough.

I'm certain that some of you are now thinking to yourself, "Where is he going with all this? Does he really have a plan to alleviate the suffering of so many millions of people?"

The answer to this question is a qualified "yes." It's qualified because, in all probability, you'll not see it in your lifetime.

It has taken generations to conceive this malaise in the emotional part of man and it will probably take generations to get it under control.

The real solution must come from the medical community, which today is concerned mainly with the body. They know little of psychosomatic illness or the close correlation of the body and the mind. But I predict that they will ultimately see the light and take steps to bring about "emotional health," not "mental health."

The medical community will come to realize that "as the twig is bent, so grows the tree," or as my father used to say, "What you learn as a child you never forget."

Thus, I see in the future "preventative emotional disorder" care with counselors for pre-kindergarten children and also for youngsters in kindergarten and grade school. Parents will get training for proper handling of childhood emotional problems and psychologists will have the great respect of all the community.

The reason all this has to come from the doctors is simple: they are so highly respected that they and only they can do it.

Few people realize the depth of these emotional problems. I have said this many times, "Everyone is neurotic, it's just a question of degree." The amelioration of these neuroses will take generations. But, it will be worth the effort, as it is one of our greatest problems.

MUCH LOVE FROM YOUR PRESUMPTUOUS OLD DAD AND G.P.

I hope you all enjoyed my "aspects of man" as much as I did writing it.

As of today, your mom and G.M. isn't doing too well, but we hope she'll get better soon.

# Looking Within

# Myself

As in me, myself, and I ... the most important person in the world to me! Now, lets take the word "myself" and divide it and examine each part.

Of course, we get MY and SELF, each important in it's own right. MY is the selfish part, as in my wife, my dog, my house, my children, my grandchildren. These are all important to ME, but not necessarily in that order.

Let's start with the infant, who is, without a doubt the greediest person on earth. He (or she) wants all the milk, because the infant knows only that this wonderful elixis is the key to his growth and survival. He (or she) doesn't know about the milk of human kindness or any form of sharing. Of course, as we grow and gain true perspective we can change and become warm, kind, generous, loving people. Unfortunately, there are those who never grow up and learn compassion.

We must always remember, though, that MY is truly important. We need the wisdom to know the importance of what is ours and to appreciate the wonders of all the things that truly belong to us.

The other part, SELF, is more exciting and intriguing because there are so many ramifications to the word. Consider this list.

| | | |
|---|---|---|
| Self contained | Self doubt | Self righteous |
| Self confident | Self conscious | Self sufficient |
| Self love | Self starter | Self incriminating |
| Self reliance | Self importance | |
| Self hate | Selfish | |

All of these words are "self-explanatory". Yet, there are several that I would like to discuss. Self love and self hate are primary factors in our lives. Just as love and hate both reside in our bodies and minds, so does the application of those feelings to ourselves. Too many people hate themselves because they do not meet the expectations of parents who want their children to be perfect. And this translates into our own expectations and we hate ourselves because we fail. On the other hand, too much self-love can be destructive as well. As usual, we find the middle road, the happy medium to be the best. If we can learn to love ourselves and at the same time forgive ourselves for our human weaknesses and foibles, we can live long and happy lives.

My most significant and satisfying mantra is "I'm counting my blessings and loving myself exactly as I am." Try it ... believe it ... love it! If you can love yourself as you are, you've won a great battle.

And, finally, I want to dwell on SELF CONFIDENCE. Here again, too much is not good, but too little is abominable.

I'll never forget the story of the reporter who was interviewing the CEO of a huge organization. They were interrupted numerous times by phone calls in which the CEO said "do this" or "do that" ... "buy this" ... "sell that", etc. After one rather long conversation the reporter said, "You're making so many decisions, one after the other. Aren't you afraid you'll make a mistake?" The CEO answered, "Oh, I make lots of mistakes. I just try to keep my average well under 50 percent."

This story illustrates true self confidence, the belief in oneslf, the feeling that all's well in my world, and that I can solve most of my problems successfully. My wish for all of you is that you have sufficient self confidence and self love to live long and happy lives.

❏ Dad,   ❏ GP,   ❏ GGP

# I Did It!

TO MY CHILDREN AND GRANDCHILDREN:

I DID IT! I DID IT! I DID IT!

What did I do that I'm so proud of? I did something that very few people do, and virtually none at my age: I COMPLETED MY ANALYSIS!

Let's go back to Decatur about 55 or 60 years ago, when your mother/GM gave me some wonderful advice. She had been to a PTA meeting where a young psychiatrist, Donald Sweazy, spoke about his work and its benefits for the patient. She told me I should go see him... that he could help me. I did - and she was right.

I learned a lot about my psyche as we began the analytic process. Unfortunately, Dr. Sweazy left Decatur for a larger city and my investigative process was put on hold for many, many years.

Now, let's go back about 15 years. I had received the last procedure on my eyes from Dr. Chen and I was legally blind, with the same peripheral vision and limited frontal vision that I have now.

Shortly after that I met a neighbor who was a psychologist. She said that I should join Paul White (another psychologist in her office) in a therapy group for men over 70. Why, I asked, should I do that? Her reply was that I was quite angry inside. She was right! I had denied my anger about my loss of sight as I had done all my life about my childhood angers. So I went to therapy and it was quite helpful in coping with my anger.

But - I also learned that I had been an angry man (inside) all of my life. Now my inquiring nature was piqued. I wanted to investigate further.

Vicki had told me about her therapist, Lynda Schmidt. I called her and we agreed to meet regularly by phone. I found out that even though she was only a psychologist, she was as good as or better than most psychiatrists.

I didn't realize that we had started the analytic process of living through the past layer by layer. By that I mean the same "living though the past" was repeated over and over - each time getting a little deeper. And each time there was more physical pain. A good example is "fear." Whenever I concentrated on my inner fears, my feet would break out in many blisters that went away when I reached some sort of resolution.

What happened this year was my release of the final layer of defense. It created a huge physical reaction. If you will recall, a few months ago I had excruciating pains in my sacroiliac. I had to go to a pain doctor three times to get shots to relieve the pain.

Then I had - one after the other - a small heart attack, congestive heart failure, and atrial fibrillation.

Doctor Lerner (my internist) and Doctor Hepp (my cardiologist) will have a hard time believing all that came from my psychic shock. They deal only with the physical but man is made up of body, mind, and spirit, according to the Buddhists. The three are interconnected and work together for our well-being… or illness.

As I write about my ordeal I ask myself if it was worth all the pain and energy that was necessary to accomplish my goal. My answer is a resounding YES!!

I may not be in the greatest health physically, but my psychic being feels cleansed. And I have learned so much about what makes me (and everyone) a functioning human being.

The five greatest lessons I have learned are: (1) love, (2) perfection, (3) gratefulness, (4) acceptance, and (5) mellowfellowness. I have written you extensively about love, perfection and gratefulness. I promise you a large dose of "acceptance" and "mellowfellowness" in subsequent issues.

MUCH LOVE -
Dad/G.P.

P.S. You have questions?? I have answers.

124

# I Am Normal

I must confess that I am NORMAL. By that, I mean that I have been emotionally ill for most of my life.

At various times, since I was 35 or 40 years old, I have had therapy. But the beginning of my real introspection came when I spent two years with a men's therapy group five to seven years ago. Ostensibly, I was there to ameliorate the anger engendered by my diminished vision, but I discovered that I had lived in anger all my life.

I then decided to dig into my psyche and worked with Vicki's and Howie's therapist, Lynda Schmidt. She's wonderful! With intermittent phone calls, she helped me put all the pieces together and now I feel that I've graduated.

In celebration, I dashed off the enclosed poem. Longfellow I'm not, but it tells my story.

My view is that everyone needs therapy. It used to be considered a disgrace, but no more. I have told many of you that I think group therapy is great, but one-to-one is really better. I strongly recommend it to all of you!!

This is the first message of the year 2002 and I'm delighted that we are all well. Since Thanksgiving, Grandma (mother) has been great. She'll never be the way she was five years ago, but she's doing wonderfully well and looking beautiful. She lost eighteen pounds.

I'm nearing the end of the page, so I'll close with great love for all of you and a wish for a happy and healthy 2002.

__Dad __G.P.

# FREEDOM

I'M FREE TO LOVE, I'M FREE TO WIN.
I'M FREE TO LET MY LIFE BEGIN.
I'M FREE TO THINK, I'M FREE TO FEEL.
I'M FREE TO KNOW WHAT'S REALLY REAL.

I'M FREE TO LOVE, I'M FREE TO HATE.
I'M FREE TO RAGE AND BE IRATE.

I'M FREE TO WIN, I'M FREE TO LOSE.
I'M FREE TO ACT THE WAY I CHOOSE.
I'LL LIVE IN LOVE INSTEAD OF HATE.
I'LL LIVE IN JOY WITH MY GREAT MATE.

I'M FREE FROM ANGST...I'M FREE FROM FEARS
THAT HAVE CRIPPLED ME ALL THESE YEARS.
I'M FREE TO SAY "GOODBYE PERFECTION"
AND, HOPEFULLY, REJECT REJECTION.

# Political Hopes

# Yesterday is History

I was flipping the dial of the TV recently when I stopped to listen to a Country Western tune called, "Yesterday Is History - Tomorrow is a Mystery." What a wonderful combination of philosophy and psychology!!

Everyone knows the old cliché, "Don't cry over spilt milk." But, we do. I play duplicate bridge and most every player is wont to say, "If I had done this or that I would have made the contract." Some players want to change the name of the game from "bridge: to "woulda, coulda, shoulda."

Speaking of bridge, there's the story about four elderly Jewish widows living in retirement. Before they started a bridge game one day they started to reminisce about their wonderful husbands who were gone. Finally, one lady said, "Vot vas vas. Deal!"

Then there are those who bemoan their fate because of a conflicted and terrible childhood. I am reminded of a conversation with my brother-in-law Hammy Loeb, about the problems of childhood. He made a pithy observation, "let's face it, everyone had a lousy childhood."

Those are just a few examples of "Yesterday is history." We could recount many others. But is there a lesson to be learned here? Of course there is. It's true that we can't change the past, but we can learn from our mistakes, or can learn to accept the reality of our past.

The bridge player who makes mistakes can use them as a lesson for improvement. The widow who said, "Deal!" was really saying they should stop dwelling on the past and get on with their lives and activities. And those persons who are truly disturbed by their childhood should get a good therapist so they can change and become happier people.

Now I want to discuss the future. "Tomorrow is a Mystery" is certainly true. On our anniversary we had a small dinner party. After dessert I told them how intrigued I was with the "history, mystery." I asked them to speak about tomorrow, the future, and what they saw for themselves, our country, and the world. I was happy to see how committed they all were to their spouses, because most of them spoke about how they envisioned themselves in the future with a happy life with their mates.

One man spoke of his concerns about the future of our country with its enormous debt and what he felt was poor leadership. I, too, deplore the spending of a "drunken sailor" as I term George W. Bush. And I honestly believe he started the Iraq war to maintain his presidency. It worked! Now, we're spending billions and billions to democratize Iraq and help the citizens of Iraq (less than the population of California) to a better life.

Yet, no matter how much we deplore the negative aspects of this Iraqi effort, there are positive factors. This is a huge step in bringing democracy to the Middle East, and, hopefully, it will spread. A friend asked me recently, "Do you know that no democracies have waged war on one another?" What a powerful statement! So, my positive crystal ball tells me that I see more and more democracies in the future.

When everyone has made their comments about "tomorrow," I sounded a somber note. I said that I was concerned about Al-Qaeda and whether they might release an atomic bomb somewhere in our country. This points to the fact that we'll always have negative factors in our lives and future generations will have to deal with them.

What else do I see in my crystal ball? I see the shift from the US to China as the most powerful nation in the world. They have the brains and the huge population of energetic people who are just starting to feel their strength. Here, too, we can hope they become a democracy so we can live in peace with them.

Of course I'm worried about the activities of nations like North Korea and Iran. But I see the powerful nations of the world who have always banded together to handle the "outlaws." Meaning cooperation of every county in a strong United Nations can accomplish miracles. Along with this could be a little sharing of the wealth. I voted for Wendell Wilkie because I loved his "One World" concept.

One of the most poignant stories I ever heard was about the teacher who

130

gave her pupil a jigsaw puzzle of the world to put together. When the youngster did it in record time, the teacher said, "How did you do it so fast?" The pupil answered, "It was easy. On the back was a picture of the man, and when the man was right, the world was right!"

I have always said that everyone is neurotic; it's just a matter of degree. I also feel that we have done little or nothing to alleviate our neuroses. This is a real challenge for the future generations: to devise methods of training people how to cope with their animal feelings, how to resolve their conflicts, how to understand their past, and how to use this knowledge for their betterment.

This is a goal to strive for! I have lived almost a century and have seen tremendous changes in medicine, nutrition, and exercise habits that have benefitted mankind greatly, but there is a huge lack of effort to improve our emotional health. My hope for the future is that we'll develop ways to help neurotic and psychotic people. Then the "world can be right because the man will be right"

I'm an old man. My days are numbered. I wish I could live for another century to see what transpires. But I can't. All I can do is say to future generations, "good luck, guys!!"

# Democratic Socialism?

I am not an economist professional. Neither am I an expert on communism, socialism, and democracy. But I have some knowledge about all of them and I consider myself an intelligent observer.

Before he died, Bob Hemond, a professor of economics, and I had long discussions about the economy. We both agreed that big trouble was coming, and we were right. The excesses of laissez-faire capitalism, with its greed and corruption, have led to a world-wide debacle. The packaging and repeated repackaging of mortgages led to escalation of home prices as anyone who is wants to buy a house with little or no down payment.

Tremendous gambling on the market brought about huge inflated values. This marks the end of capitalism as we knew it, because government had to step in and save the economy from complete collapse.

Let's pause a moment and look at communism and socialism. Communism is the most ideal form of government. From each, according to his ability; to each, according to his need. That's a beautiful concept... but it won't work. It doesn't take into account the greed that is in everyone to some degree. To say that Russia and China are communist countries is a misnomer. They are fascist states that still operate with capitalism. Socialism, on the other hand, still works for the common good in a framework of economic effort that allows for greater individual achievement.

We have had limited socialism for a long time. The best examples are Social Security, Medicare, and Medicaid. Our police forces and fire departments also work for the welfare of everyone.

We are now looking to government for complete health care, control of energy and environment, as well as control of banking and all fiscal activity. We need government to work on our infrastructure repairs to our roads and bridges. We must also get involved with the needs of our states. Almost all of them are cutting back on important items in their budgets because they are insolvent.

Then there are jobs, jobs, jobs!! We need our government to step into the economic picture so that every man or woman who wants to work will have that opportunity.

When you combine all those huge responsibilities with "oversight," which means "control," we have SOCIALISM. There will be those who deny it, looking back to the "good old days" of capitalism. In fact, many people erroneously equate democracy with capitalism.

We can still be a democracy and have socialism. I think we are trending toward a great improvement in our wealth management, our health management, and our overall well-being.

# Condoleezza Rice

*Condoleezza Rice*
*Isn't very nice*
*She causes such a blight*
*Because she is so right*
*And works with all her might*
*To keep young George uptight*
*She'll never see the light*
*'Cause she has no insight*
*It's a shame that she's so bright*
*Or – am I being trite?*

It's unfortunate that Mrs. Rice is such a reactionary Republican, because I applaud the concept of a black woman as our Secretary of State. Perhaps some day a woman, or a Jew might be our President.

It's true that our major national progress has been made by our liberal party, the Democrats. I refer to abortion rights, and, most importantly, Medicare and Social Security. All these advancements are pure socialism (which is good) and were fought bitterly by the Republicans. Their major goal is to cut taxes and run up a huge national debt.

But – the Democrats will be back in power some day and will have a chance to make more progress. Another socialistic measure is out biggest concern – complete health coverage.

This, of course will be very costly, unless the drug companies and medical community can be enlisted to join the fight for a wonderful goal.

The biggest socialized problem is to have a job for every person willing to work and because the large corporations make money only when their workforce is slim and viable. However, that too can be handled.

You can see by my comments that I am a Democratic Socialist. I know that our country has been innovative and has prospered with laissez-faire capitalism, but I am convinced that we can have strong entrepreneurship mixed with the progressive measures that will make life easier and better for everyone.

I deplore the trend toward "the haves" and the "have-nots" and the loss of a strong middle class.

# The Lights Went Out

There was a power outage in Sarasota recently that affected my home and 1,619 others. It was around 5 o'clock and the initial message from FPL was that it would be repaired by 7:15. They were wrong by 10 hours... it was 5:12 in the morning when I saw all the lights that I had turned on burning brightly. It was a glorious sight.

What did I do those 12 hours? Well, the first thing I did was to eat a cold supper. Later, I slept intermittently until 5:12 and then I slept well until 7. But mostly I did a lot of thinking... which, of course, prompts me to write this piece.

My first thoughts were about our attitude toward the necessities of life. We take for granted the electric power, our constant flow of good, clean water, plenty of good food, friendships, love, good entertainment, and all the things that are important to lead a complete life.

Then I thought of all the people in the world who don't have all of the above. I thought of the Iraqis whose lives we have wrecked. They don't have good, clean water, enough electricity, and probably not enough food. They live in terror, as do so many who fear our 21st century great invention of "suicide bombers."

I thought of Thoreau who said that "the masses lead lives of quiet desperation." That quote has such great application today, long after the author died. The news is filled with misery. In fact, that's about all you hear on the TV news shows. Here are some examples:

> Marines kill 24 Iraqis in cold blood.
> Over 6,000 killed in earthquake in Java.
> 200,000 to 300,000 left homeless by the same earthquake, their homes ruined.
> Nine huge hurricanes predicted for this year.
> One out of every three Americans is obese.
> A man throws his two children out a 15-story window in Miami – then himself.

Entire family is killed by a thief.
2,000,000 die of AIDS every year (our worthy you-know-who said the solution was "abstinence." He'd probably advise those with lung problems to stop breathing)...

It goes on and on, without letup.

I'm sitting here now... ruminating about what I have just written. It sounds gloomy and pessimistic, which of course, is not me. I'm really optimistic about the future of the world. We lived through WWII and survived the machinations of a Hitler, who almost ruled the world. And we picked up the pieces after 9/11, even though many lives were destroyed, and the people of New Orleans are working hard to achieve some semblance of good living.

As an optimist, I live in hope that we'll have a better world. Perhaps Al Gore's book on global warming will propel him into the presidency, where he or some other good man or woman can right the wrongs of the present administration.

The only Republican I voted for as president was Wendell Wilkie, because he had a vision of "One World" that was thrilling and exciting. The only way for world-wide peace and happiness is for the people of the world to walk together... to stop killing one another in senseless wars.

Perhaps we can live in hope - not fear. And perhaps we can heed the admonition of the ancient Hebrews who promulgated the wonderful command: LOVE THY NEIGHBOR AS THY SELF. The lights came back on Bird Key. Let's hope they come back (figuratively) all over the world.


P.S. I'm very close to a 90-year-old man who walks his dog every morning on Bird Key. He was heard to mutter something that sounded like "all is well, so what the hell!"

# "Yes We Can"

When we watched the wonderful Democratic Convention, the sound of "Yes we can" reverberated throughout that huge stadium repeatedly during the four days.

This rang a bell with me as I have been thinking a lot about the importance of the mind and its strength. I recall that Reverend Norman Vincent Peale wrote a book in the middle of the last century called "The Power of Positive Thinking." It was enormously successful because it had great meaning for everyone.

I must admit that I have been a positive thinker all my life. Here are a few examples: I was so confident when I opened my second store in Decatur in 1954. The fact that there were plenty of furniture stores in Decatur and the possibility of failure never entered my mind. I did more than make a living with that store.

Then I recall a developer friend, Ken Huston, saying "Let's buy the lease on that mobile home park." I was the so-called "money man" in the deal. We bought it, moved all the trailers off, and built a restaurant and a building for retail stores and offices. That positive thinking led to what is known today as "Cohn Family Partnership"... a Trust for all my children and grandchildren.

My best example is when I joined six others and said "YES WE CAN" build a Jewish retirement center and assisted care facility. The Jewish Federation couldn't help because the project was too vast. We had no money... just an idea. I called on a few friends and we raised the seed money to start the project.

This positive thinking led to the building of Kobernick House and Anchin Pavilion.

So, what is the power of positive thinking, and why is it so powerful? I think it is the power of love. In my opinion, love is the most powerful force in the universe. Love is totally positive, while hate is completely negative. Positive thinking is a loving feeling that promotes positive actions and positive results.

A simple example is my relationship with Ruth. I love her and she loves me. This power has propelled us into a happy life as we enjoy our "senior" senior years. Her family and mine are very similar. She has three children; I have three children. She has two grand-  sons and three granddaughters; I have two grandsons and three grand-daughters. The power of love and positive thinking of the Patriarch and Matriarch has been transmitted to these two families. I see in all of them a great lovingness, good relationships with each other, and a lot of pro-ductivity. That's good positive thinking.

On a larger scale, there is love for humanity, the kind of love that makes people yearn to help their fellow man. This is the love that the Democrats mean when they shout repeatedly, "Yes we can!"

We can use this power in our own lives. We can love ourselves, which is most important, as well as others. We can make a difference by living our lives in lovingness.

Let us help President Obama move mountains as he and the new admin-istration work to bring about change in healthcare, education, environ-ment, energy, and the economy. Above all, we should use our power of positive thinking as we say:

YES WE CAN - make a difference!!

Love, Dad, GP, GGP

My Life

# My Life — 1916 - 20??

I must be getting egotistical in my old age, but I thought you'd like to know about my life - with insightful commentary along the way. No naysayers, please.

This is a rough outline:

I  PRE-NATAL
    A.  Harry Cohn and family
    A2.  The Glasses
    B.  The Rosenbergs
    C.  The Woolfs
    D.  Ida and Louis

II  MY LIFE IN COLLINSVILLE

III  MY LIFE IN ST. LOUIS

IV  MY LIFE IN GILLESPIE

VI  EARLY LIFE IN TAYLORVILLE

VII  MY LIFE AT U of ILLINOIS

If you followed the Roman numerals, you'll find that I omitted #V. That is:

V  LIFE IN PANA

Going on in the chapters:

VIII EARLY LIFE WITH MOTHER/GM
    A.  Courtship
    B.  Marriage and honeymoon
    C.  Life in Taylorville
    D.  The big explosion and aftermath

IX LIFE IN CHICAGO

X LIFE IN DECATUR
   A. Early Years
   B. 777 S. Monroe
   C. The second store
   D. The mobile home park
   E. LINCOLN MANOR
   F. Heart attack and its effect on me
   G. Roger Rosenkranz

XI LIFE IN SARASOTA
   A. Midsummer Lakes
   B. 510 BLUE JAY PLACE
   C. Business and commercial ventures

If I live long enough to finish this, there will be much more.

MUCH LOVE -

Dad/G.P.

Ida and Louis Cohn....

# *Prenatal*

## COHNS

Hershel Cohn, my grandfather, came to America with his wife, Sonya. Her maiden name was Rosenberg. He sold merchandise from a pack on his back in the Collinsville-Belleville area. Later, when he had become more affluent, he and his partner, Morris Glass, opened a general store in Collinsville. Sonya was a very good businessperson and she worked in the store also.

They had a son, Louis, and a daughter, Sadie, and then Hershel died, leaving Sonya, pregnant with Uncle Harry, to raise her family. Later she would marry her partner, Morris Glass. My father was twelve years old at the time and he opposed the marriage. Shades of Freud! Grandpa Glass was a wonderful man - more about him later.

Uncle Harry was very bright, became a successful divorce lawyer, and married one of his clients, Aunt Elinor, after years of being a playboy in Chicago; they had two children, Morgan and Sharon.

Aunt Sadie, one of the sweetest persons I have ever met, married Abe Cohen, a druggist, and had one child, Herbert. More about them later.

Grandpa Morris and Grandma Glass had only one child, Jerry, who married Valma Yarwitz. Their children, Stan, Carol, and Mark, are all part of our lives.

## GLASSES

Grandma Glass had a son, Henry, by a previous marriage. My father had a brother, a step-brother, and a half-brother. Henry had two daughters, Shirley (about my age) and Phyllis. I don't think Grandpa Glass was the greatest businessman in the world. I felt that Grandma was the power. She would say, "Glaazz" in a strong voice, and he would comply with her wishes. Control persons go way back in our family. But, as I've always said in their defense, control persons are the "do-ers" of the world.

Grandpa Glass loved all the grandchildren and promised each one a pink, yellow, green, or any other color pony when they went to his mythical farm. He was wonderful, as was Grandma Glass, despite her Rosenberg authoritarianism.

ROSENBERGS

Grandma Glass had a brother, who was called "Uncle" by the entire family. He was a dour individual who produced two children with his first wife, and four with his second wife, known always as "Aunt Esther" to all. Max, the first boy had a successful ladies' ready-to-wear business. The second child, Bertha, was a real character. She was an old maid, who worked at Garlands in St. Louis and learned everything there was to learn about anything and everything. She always looked like she was eating a green persimmon.

Aunt Esther was a jovial, rotund lady who was loved by everyone. She produced three daughters, Ceil, Lee, and Della. Ceil married Joe Hochman; they had two children, Shirley and Bernard. Lee, a real beauty, married mother's brother, Lou and they had two daughters, Riselle and Harriette. Riselle died when she was quite young. Della, a dour Rosenberg, married a Swedish newspaperman named Karlsson. They had two children, Merwyn and Bunner. Aunt Esther also had a son, Bennie, who lived with her in Chicago until his untimely death in his forties or fifties.

The most important Rosenberg was the "matriarch" Bubby, who lived in St. Louis. She lost one eye, lived to be 100 years old, and regaled everyone with stories about the "old country."

The story about my father and Bubby was told again and again. Everyone spoke Yiddish, so when Bubby had asked dad about Nellie, the horse, he told her that Nellie died. When she asked him why, he said "Zie bist an Alta, ah-zay du." Translation: "She was an old one - just like you!"

146

## WOOLFS

Isaac Woolf was Itsak Velvel Luchansky when he and his wife arrived at Ellis Island with three small children. Ida was two years old at the time. Velvel is "wolf" in Yiddish, so the immigration officials, for the sake of convenience, dropped the last name and made him a "Wolf." Later, Uncle Joe added a zero to make the name less animalistic.

Uncle Joe was the oldest. He was very bright and earned a PhD degree in Philosophy at the noted University of Chicago. Lou, also very bright, was a marvelous bridge player, and married Lee Rosenberg, a distant cousin. Joe married Aunt Augusta, who produced Ruthmary and David. My mother, Ida, grew up like a little princess, with her father and two brothers as her loving constituents. Later she became a Queen, with an admiring husband, three children, and nine grandchildren who adored her.

This discussion of the Woolfs leads me into the next segment, Ida and Louis, but before I do that, I want to point out that I remember all the relatives I have written about and many others, because we were a close family and had a lot of family parties. That was our big entertainment. I remember when Dad and I visited Chicago, he took me to see all the relatives and even close family friends.

## IDA AND LOUIS

The Woolfs came to Collinsville/St. Louis to visit the Cohn/Glass/Rosenberg clan when mother was twelve years old. Grandpa Woolf was a second or third cousin of Grandma Glass, which made my parents slightly related.

Dad fell madly in love with Mother and vowed that he would marry her. Since he was a man of honor, he kept his promise and they were married on October 18th, 1914, when he had just turned 22 years old and Mother was 21 ½ years old. They had a super honeymoon at Starved Rock Park, Illinois, and then went to Collinsville to live. Their next big mutual effort was to create a gorgeous little baby boy - ME!!!

Gershom

# The Early Years Collinsville, St. Louis, Gillespie

## CHAPTER II – COLLINSVILLE -

My father owned and operated a small men's haberdashery. He had been in the family general store all his life and retailing was in his blood. After he completed the eighth grade, he went to business school for two years, and then he went into the store. He was accomplished in bookkeeping and typing... typed his own letters.

He and my mother rented a small apartment in the home of a lovely large German woman, Mrs. Esterlein. There, mother cooked wonderful meals on a coal range and, after I emerged, her main job was caring for me.

I was a beautiful baby (have the pictures to prove it) and spoke early, but very slowly. The oft repeated story about my very early childhood was when I was walking down the street with an old watch that someone had given to me. A neighbor, Mrs. Thompson, saw me and asked, "Gershom, does your watch run?" I immediately replied in a slow drawl, "No, Mrs. Thompson, I have to carry it." This, of course, was an early sign of future genius.

I was too young to remember Collinsville, but I'm certain, as the first grandchild, I was idolized by Grandma and Grandpa Glass, as well as Aunt Sadye and Uncle Jerry, who were still at home.

I have been told that I was driven with a horse and buggy when we went to St. Louis to see my great-grandmother, Bubby. Collinsville is now a bedroom community for St. Louis - a half-hour drive. It took hours by horse and buggy.

# CHAPTER III – ST. LOUIS -

I have to assume that my father's haberdashery business failed after a few years, because he took a job with Scudder-Gale selling wholesale groceries. That is when we moved to St. Louis, headquarters for Scudder-Gale. We lived on Maple Avenue, not too far from Aunt Sadye, who had married a druggist, Uncle Abe.

Our lives were somewhat intertwined with theirs as Aunt Sadye and mother were great friends. Uncle Abe was an accomplished pianist, and he always played for us when we visited them.

His brother, Izzy, was a wonderful violinist and became an excellent orchestra conductor. After he married Ethel Talbot, a fine English pianist, he changed his name to Irving Talbot, and wound up as a conductor for Paramount Studios. He was highly regarded because of his precision which was so important then, when the music had to be played as the picture was being filmed.

Uncle Abe's mother and father were sweet old Orthodox Jews. Mr. Cohen was the Shamas at the Shul and Mrs. Cohen was a marvelous cook. We had many wonderful meals at their home, always topped off with Tageloch, a sweet, hard, Jewish pastry. This was Mrs. Cohen's specialty. I never had it before or since.

Aunt Sadye and Uncle Abe had one child, Herbert, who was two years younger than I. A couple of years ago, Herb wrote me a poignant letter with his reminiscences about our early childhood. He reminded me about how I taught him to use the bed as a trampoline...and how that eventually led to his falling and breaking an arm.

We also went to his dad's drug store and acted as soda jerks at the fountain. But our biggest "coup" was going to the streetcar depot on Hodamont Avenue. Then we went from car to car, clanging the bells, and getting some of them to move a little.

Uncle Jerry visited us quite often as he had a good friend in St. Louis, Eli Feldman, a shoe salesman. I can remember them building a radio from a kit that they purchased. It worked! And I remember going to school not far from our home.

But the big event in our lives in St. Louis was the advent of sister Estelle who came into our lives December 30, 1921. Of course, I had mixed feelings about her, but eventually I came to accept her. She was very pretty and didn't give us too much trouble.

## CHAPTER IV – ON TO GILLESPIE...

In 1923 Uncle Rosenberg died, and my dad jumped at the opportunity to get back into retailing. He had no money but he bought the ready-to-wear store for $5,000 with his promise to pay Aunt Esther $50 per month until the debt was paid...including interest. My father was an extremely generous man, as he paid Aunt Esther that $50 every month until she died, because she needed the money. Don't forget, $50 then was like $500 now!

Getting back to the move, mom and dad and I went to Gillespie in the summer of 1923, leaving Estelle to stay with Aunt Sadye. Gillespie was a small, sleepy town of four to five thousand people. Coal mining was the chief occupation. It was in Illinois about fifty miles from St. Louis. Most of the residents were Scottish.

Dad changed the name of the store to COHN'S CASH STORE and I worked with the helpers to string up socks so they could be pulled off as wanted. This was my first experience in a store and I loved it.

We lived in the back of the store because we didn't have enough money to rent a house. My mother, God love her, made the most marvelous dinners, cooking on a two burner hot plate. It was great family togetherness, and the intruder, Estelle, was not there to spoil it.

The business was fairly successful and, in the fall, we rented a very nice home, across from the school I would attend. I had completed 1 ½ years of school in St. Louis, but they tested me and put me in 3rd grade. Thus I was always ahead of my class two-thirds of a year.

As I think back, I remember Wilson Renner, an "older" boy with whom I became friendly. He was not too smart...behind in school by a couple of years...he smoked...and he knew about S-E-X!!

In fact, he organized a sex party with Dewayne Fox, his two step-sisters, Irma and Marie, and Dewayne's real sister, Clara, and me. He took Irma into the asparagus path at Dewayne's house, along with Dewayne and Marie. Clara and I wound up in the shed. I don't know what the others did, but little Clara and I had a wonderful time talking in the shed. My first sexperience at nine or ten years of age!!

Then I remember James Gaddie, a real no-good-nik who tripped me as I was running out of the middle school I attended. I fell and hurt my knee. The doctor put it into a cast. When my parents told Uncle Abe about it, he insisted that we come to St. Louis to see a doctor there. We did and this doctor, a specialist, took the cast off with the awful prediction that if the cast had remained, I would have had a stiff leg for the rest of my life. My lucky star was burning brightly.

The Jewish community in Gillespie was quite small. The Browns were the local shoe repair people. They had two daughters, Ethel and Bernice. Armand Sherman was the "rich Jew." He and his brother in Staunton owned department stores. Then there was a junk dealer and dear friends of my folks', the Riches, who had a shoe store. They had a son, Maury, about Estelle's age. We visited with them a lot.

We lived in Gillespie for eight years, but the last three years were exciting for my dad because he went into the furniture business. Sam Hiken, an old friend from Collinsville had two stores, Collinsville and Edwardsville. He came to dad and proposed another one, a partnership with my father in Gillespie.

This store was called H&C FURNITURE and gave new dimension to our lives. All was well until Sam Hiken began sending all the slow-selling merchandise from his Edwardsville store without discounting them.

This broke up their friendship, their partnership, and our life in Gillespie.

More about that next month.

To wind up Gillespie, I finished grade school there, went to high school two years before we moved, and led a very quiet life as a kid growing up in a small town.

But the big news was the crash in 1929 and with it, the birth of little baby sister, Francy. She's been a constant source of explosiveness and volatility, just as the business climate was at that time.

# Next Move
# Pana, Illinois

In the last chapter on "Gillespie," I wrote that my father had a big fight with his partner in H&C Furniture Co. and, with his meager capital (after they settled), set out to find a furniture store to buy. Remember - this was 1931, two years after the crash, and in the middle of the worst depression ever for the U.S. He found one in Pana, a city of six thousand called the "City of Roses" because it had two large greenhouses, amling and maton, which shipped roses all over the world.

This store was built for and operated as a furniture store by Mr. Eilers. It had a large basement, main floor, and the second floor was divided. The back half was a part of the furniture store, the front half was offices. We used the offices as a home. I know this sounds weird but it was actually very nice.

Picture a stairway on the left leading up from the street. As you come up you enter a foyer which was formerly a waiting room. There you see a wood burning stove for nighttime heating, when the store's furnace was set on low. Of course - no air conditioning. There was a bathroom with a tub and, facing the stairs next to the bathroom, a large room which became a bedroom for Francy, Estelle, and a wonderful girl who came with us from Gillespie as our maid. She was Martha Wojtkieucz, a Polish name, pronounced vith-cay-vich. She ultimately left us to marry her boyfriend, Tony.

To complete the house layout, the three rooms facing the street were the dining room, living room, and master bedroom. The kitchen was in front of the dining room, opposite the stairs, and my room was a small room behind the living room. It had probably been a large storage room.

We were in the midst of a depression, but we felt no pain. No one had a "pot to pee in or a window to throw it out" as an old saying goes, but we were happy. Francy, the baby, played with her girlfriend Jennie behind

154

the store and in the alley. Jennie lived across the alley. Her father was a mechanic and had a garage which fronted on the ally.

When I discussed Pana with my sister, Estelle, she said she had no memory of Pana at all... it was just a blur for her. She was twelve years old when we came to Pana, and we lived there for about four years. That was hard for me to understand, because my memories of Pana are extremely vivid.

The summer of 1931, when we moved to Pana, was a time of great physical growth for me. I was extremely small for my age until then. Suddenly, I sprouted and became the size of many of my peers. It was then that I discovered GIRLS! I met Clarice Shafer and Ann Slaymaker when I went to play tennis. Clarice was a senior in high school as I became a junior and Ann was in my class. We were just "tennis buddies."

But when I went to school at good old Pana High, I was smitten by a pretty blonde freshman, Sue Endris. She was the daughter of an Italian Catholic Deputy Sheriff and she liked me a lot. On our first date, I kissed her good night on the cheek. She laughed, and then taught me how to kiss. It was fantastic... a lesson which I've never forgotten. After she gave me her picture with some sentimental wording on it that Christmas, my mother became worried that we would grow up together and eventually marry. She set out to break us up - and succeeded. However, that was the only time she and dad interfered in my dating and/or love life.

Sue and I met again about thirty years ago. She bought some living room furniture from our Decatur store. Our birthdays are March 4th and March 5th. So from then on, we either sent cards or phoned at birthday time. She is now in a nursing home with Alzheimer's disease, and will probably not live much longer.

I was always a "one woman man" and had a series of romances with Elizabeth Alderson, Doris Beyers, Luanna Werner, and Mary Jones - who visited her grandparents in nearby Assumption. This practice continued in college until I met my true love. Actually, it has continued all my life.

Getting back to Pana, I had a very close friend, Kenny Snow. We spent a lot of time together... listened a lot to Isham Jones band which played on radio station WLW in Cincinnati... and we smoked a lot... a practice Kenny never broke. He died of emphysema a few years ago.

Other male friends included Curtis Tuppero, Maurice Clayton, Jake Levine, John Detlow, and Robert Reed. Curt worked at his dad's cigar store where we played poker and shot craps in the back room. Maurice was a motorcycle "jock" and a very genial guy. I played tennis with John a lot, and I have a funny story to relate about Robert Reed in the next chapter.

My last two years of high school were at Pana High. The teachers were excellent and I was a good student. Louie Tanner, whose parents owned a junk yard and the Palace Theater, and I were co-salutatorians when we graduated. Zola Dickerson, a real drone, was valedictorian. Louie and I were roommates our first two years at Illinois. He was quite bright, became a good lawyer, and married his cousin Bertha, who was his only girlfriend. He died eight years ago.

Let's get back to the store. I loved the furniture business. I was a part-time salesman and part-time delivery helper. I worked on Saturdays, and sometimes after school, and during the summer. John Guinee was our salesman, and Floyd Strivers, a high school football hero, was the driver. I remember selling coal ranges, old fashioned round coal heaters, wood burning stoves, and ice boxes.

The big turning point in our lives came when I was on the floor early in the summer between my freshman and sophomore years in college. A man came in and asked for Mr.. Cohn. When I told him my dad was out, he told me why he came. His firm had bought out Bulpitt's furniture store in Taylorville because it was going broke. They ran a "Going Out of Business" sale for a long time, and now wanted to sell us the balance of the inventory that was left and get out.

I became so excited. I knew this was a golden opportunity for us and I begged him to come back in one hour when my dad would return. He did... and we made a deal. After moving a few items from our store to augment the depleted stock, we continued the sale. I went there every day and was so successful that we decided to move our store to Taylorville.

When I was doing more business in Taylorville, with a limited inventory, than he was doing in Pana with a full stock of goods, it became apparent that our future was in Taylorville. Pana was a sleepy town of six thousand. Taylorville was ten thousand, the county seat of Christian County, and most importantly, had four large Peabody coal mines in the area which brought large expendable income to the community. I wanted to quit school and become a partner with my dad. Both parents were adamant! I had to finish college and decide whether to become a lawyer or a furniture man.

You'll learn my decision in the next chapter.

MUCH LOVE -

Dad

# 3 1/2 Years at University of Illinois

Before I begin the U of I days, I would like to recall a few more people in Gillespie. In the fourth grade, I met and fell in love with Mildred Stewart. She had big, brown eyes and brunette bangs and, of course, never knew of our romantic involvement.

Then there were John Wentmore and John Roberts. The former was just a friend, but the latter and I were very close. We were the "brainy" ones who made all A's.

I think I wrote before that my father was a staunch member of B'nai B'rith, a Jewish organization with a dual purpose: to help Jews everywhere and to provide a venue for socialization.

At a banquet at the Hotel Orlando in Decatur, my parents attended a regional B'nai B'rith meeting. They came home all aglow with news about a gorgeous blonde, daughter of Lee and Fanny Greerman, who lived in Champaign. Since I was going to school there in a few months, I must look her up. In Yiddish, this is called a "Shidach."

Yes, I met her...she was cute...and I dated her most of my freshman year. We drifted apart near the end of the year and I saw very little of her subsequently. I must have made some kind of impression on her, because after she married, she had two daughters and named them Sylvia and Arlene!!

FRESHMAN YEAR:
In my freshman year, I lived with Lewie Tanner. You'll recall that he and I were co-salutatorians and that his parents owned the only picture show in town and a junk yard. We lived on Illinois Street in Urbane, very close to the campus. Our room in this large home was a choice. It was large, second floor, facing the street. In the back bedroom upstairs were Chuck Olsen, a reserve half back on the football team, and Andy Dahl, a tackle

on the first team. The family lived downstairs in the back, while the small front bedroom was occupied by Chuck Moffit, who played the saxophone. He was good...played "gigs" on the weekend. He was from Tolono, a small town near Champaign...the football players were from Chicago.

I had a good year scholastically, as I liked the required freshman courses... made Beta Sigma Chi the first semester, the equivalent of Phi Beta Kappa. But I never did well after that until my senior year. More about that later.

Lewie and I each paid eleven dollars per month for our room; tuition was $37.50 per semester. My entire 3 ½ years cost me $1,000. I was rushed by several fraternities but we couldn't afford them.

## SOPHOMORE YEAR
Lewie and I joined Dan Murray, from Pana, and Jerry David, a weirdo from Chicago, in a basement apartment (lower level) in Champaign. You stepped down three to four steps from the street. With four guys at four desks and different bedtime hours, it wasn't easy to study. As I look back, I realize that I didn't care about my major, poli-sci. Political Science was the major of choice for pre-legal students, and I know now that I didn't want to be a lawyer. I made B's and C's in Poli-Sci, but I found other courses that turned me on. I loved Philosophy and got A's in all my philosophy courses. That was my minor, along with speech.

Which brings me to my second semester and a course in debating. There I met Carl Weinberger, who became my best friend for sixty-seven years. We debated together in intramural debates, and decided to live together the following year. More about that later.

Now I have to backtrack for another lifelong friend, Ezra Ressman. E and I were short, and in ROTC, a required course for freshmen, we lined up with the tallest boys in the center, and, going left and right, to the shortest one. E turned to me and said, "Lantzman," a Yiddish word meaning fellow Jew. We shook hands and became fast friends until his premature death in his early forties. He and his friend Charlotte Growe visited us often in Decatur.

Getting back to my sophomore year, my romantic interest was a girl from East St. Louis, Sarah Lee Novak. I don't know how I met her, but we were mostly good friends with mutual intellectual interests. She was a sorority girl (H-E-DHI) and dated an independent living in a basement! I must have been a good salesman...shades of the future. Sarah Lee was my date the following year at the ballroom where I was introduced to Carl's date... some girl from Chicago named Sylvia Hechtman. More about that later... much more.

Meanwhile back at the ranch, I mean the furniture stores, Dad had sold the Pana store and opened one in Taylorville on the southwest corner of the Square. The County Courthouse was in the center and it was surrounded by four blocks of business known as "the Square." The store did well and, at the age of forty-two, my father started to make money. Both Estelle and Francy went to U of I also, but they joined S.D.T. - a very nice sorority. I was going to joke about that but, honestly, I was never jealous. I always loved my "independent" status, particularly my third year...coming up now.

JUNIOR YEAR:
When I met Carl, he was living with Ray and Ben Leland in an apartment in Champaign. Both Roy and Ben were studying Sanitary Engineering and wound up working for the City of Chicago. Ben was a senior and, near the end of the year, married his Zelda. It was difficult but they managed. Carl suggested that he, Ray, Allen Telzer, and I rent an apartment for what was his senior year and my junior year.

We found a wonderful one in Urbana in the 700 block of West Elm. This was quite a distance from the campus, so we all bought bicycles. We got along quite well...with the exception of Telzer (we called him "Helzel," Yiddish for the neck of the chicken). Luckily, he dropped out of school after the first semester.

The highlight of the year came when we were notified by Leon Rubin, a friend of Carl's, from Gillman, Illinois. Leon was excited about a girl he met at a dance. He said, "This girl has a fantastic personality and she's a marvelous dancer." She was the Sylvia Hechtman I referred to before.

Carl had gone with only one girl in his life, Lee Turen, who lived in Chicago. They had broken up shortly before Leon's visit and Carl became excited. He wanted a date with the fantastic Sylvia Hechtman.

Since his experience with "women" was so limited, he asked me to call Sylvia to make a date for him. I agreed because it was a challenge.

So, I called, told Sylvia that I was Carl Weinberger and I persuaded her to go to a ballroom with me (him). The phone call is a long story. Those of you who haven't heard it can get the "long version" from the young lady herself. She loves to tell it.

On to the ballroom... a popular place for young couples on campus. It was midterm and I had a date with my friend, Sarah Lee. I met S.H. as she danced by with Carl and wasn't terribly impressed. She was a good dancer, though.

In the meantime, she and Carl had a few more dates, but had to stop, as Carl and Lee had "made up." Sylvia, who had visited us in the apartment, became a good friend of Ray, Carl and me. Carl would wheel her to the apartment on the handlebar of his bike from the Commerce Building about three to four miles away. He would yell up to Ray and me, "put another cup of water in the soup," as he neared the apartment. We ate TALL BOY soup...an extra-large can which cost ten cents.

I became Sylvia's confidante as she told me all about the boys she dated. She did a huge juggling act, as she had four or five on the string.

That year, 1936, was a "leap year," and Sylvia's big problem was the Fine Arts Ball. Whom should she take? The selection of any one of her boyfriends would be dangerous. So, she decided to be safe and take me. I suppose our friendship had grown so much that I became concerned about that date. I had always been the "older man" giving advice to this younger friend, but a date with her was another matter. I told Ray and Carl, "I don't know if I should go to the Fine Arts Ball with Sylvia. I'm afraid I'll fall in love with her and marry her and I don't know if I want to marry her."

My worst fear was confirmed. I did fall in love with her and we did marry two years later. That night, April 4th, 1936, was spent "necking" at the top of the circular stairs in the Fine Arts building. We never did dance. The next night, we were in the sunroom of the apartment...necking again... and I said, "You know you're going to marry me," and she agreed immediately.

There we were...stretched out on the daybed...she was sixteen and I was nineteen...as we casually made the most important decision of our lives. It was the beginning of a wonderful, loving relationship that has lasted over sixty-six years!!

In my junior year I made the big decision to become a business man instead of a lawyer. I really liked the furniture business. It was fun, and besides, it gave me the opportunity to exercise my persuasive ability. This attribute is essential in everything we do, but it's most important selling "big ticket" items.

And truthfully, I wanted to marry your mother/grandmother and settle down with her and have a family.

SENIOR YEAR:
Since I lacked only eighteen credit hours to graduate, I did it in one semester of my senior year. I took twenty hours, selecting only the courses I loved, and did very well. I think the score was two hours of B and 18 - A. You can always do better when your heart is in it.

You'll have to wait for the next issue to see if my plan worked out.

# Pre-Marital Stuff

Since this chapter covers the time between our engagement and our marriage, I'm going to start with some comments about your Mother/Grandmother.

As you know, she is a very special and unique woman. I'm convinced that she, as I, received too much love...and...too much hate... from her parents in her early years. The defining moment in her life came with the death of her mother when she was nine years old. She was so traumatized by that death that she would get migraine headaches when we went to funerals. This problem has tapered off.

But there they were: Sylvia was nine years old, her brother Babe was thirteen years old, and her brother Sam was fifteen years old. Morris, her father, worked long hours at the hat factory, so the three grew up like Topsy. Sam, who was a brilliant student, never finished high school and he and Babe played with other boys, ignoring their sister, unless commanded by Morris to take her someplace.

Your Mother/Grandmother spent a lot of time alone in the house... not daring to answer the doorbell...because her father told her the Jewish Orphan Society would come and get her. She was an omnivorous reader... even read the dictionary on the advice of an older friend of the family.

She was so bright that she skipped 2 ½ years of school, finishing high school at the age of 15 ½ years. Since the University of Illinois required a chaperone at that age, she waited and entered in the fall of 1935.

She developed physically as well as mentally and dated in high school. I still kid her about the comment in her yearbook by a boy who wrote "You're sure a great kisser!" On one occasion at the U of I, Carl and I had taken Sylvia back to West Residence Hall where she lived. This was in the "friendship" period. As we left, an old high school classmate of hers said, "What are you doing with a sixteen year old kid?" She had told us she was eighteen years old... which is understandable.

During her first semester when Carl, Ray, and I didn't know her, she formed many friendships… mostly with men. In the last chapter, I wrote about my early role as counselor, advising her how best to juggle these four or five men who were enamored of her. Her schoolwork was excellent! She made Alpha Lamda Delta her first semester. This is the equivalent of Phi Beta Kappa for freshmen.

This brings us to the end of her first semester when she, Carl, Ray, and I became very good friends and to my entry as her lover and our verbal engagement on our second date.

Your Mother/Grandmother planned to return to school for her sophomore (my senior) year, but a terrible event occurred: her father was in a huge automobile accident returning from Milwaukee and almost died. He was in a coma for months. So Sylvia, Sam, and Babe (his real name was Irving) had to run the hat factory. Ultimately, Sam wound up with the business, while Babe and your Mother/Grandmother got other jobs. Although your Mother/Grandmother went to college only one year, she is brighter than 99% who graduate. That, of course, is my opinion.

So….this bright young lady decided to get a job. On her first interview, she was hired as the office person for Olson Kehl Submerged Water Heaters for $15.00 per week. Her only other job prior to our marriage was with Schwartz Coin Machines. Gladys Reisman, the older sister of her close friend Sylvia Reisman was the office manager. When Gladys left, your Mother/Grandmother got her job. She earned $25.00 per week in that capacity plus splitting all the coins left in the slot machines with the foreman. Shade of things to come with one of our progeny! Incidentally, $25.00 then is equivalent to $600 to $700 today.

Meanwhile, back at the farm, I mean the furniture store in Taylorville, Bernie Kalis and I were the sales team and I really enjoyed selling. This, of course, was after my last semester at U of I.

I missed my Sylvia a lot. Since the end of her freshman (my junior) year, we saw one another infrequently when I had time off to drive to Chicago. Uncle Jerry and his brother-in-law Herman Yawitz were in Chicago on business. They knew how lonesome I was, so they kidnapped your Mother/Grandmother for a weekend trip to Taylorville. They dropped her off on their way to Collinsville/St. Louis. My mother thought she was a "hussy" to visit a man she wasn't even formally engaged to. That situation was soon rectified at an engagement party on my 21st birthday with all the family present. Grandma Glass brought two diamond earrings with her from Europe. She gave one to Herb Cohn and one to me for engagement rings.

I must backtrack a bit to relate a wonderful story about your Mother/Grandmother the first time she visited us in Taylorville. Carl Weinberger's father was a wonderful man with a great sense of humor. He told your Mother/Grandmother not to worry about going to Taylorville. He told her to ignore the pigs and chickens in the yard at the Cohn house when she arrived and not to be shocked by the huge red flowers in the rugs in the living room, plus a few more negatives. Of course, none of it was true, but the point is: SHE CAME ANYHOW!!

Coincidentally, we have just discovered two boxes of letters in the hall credenza. They are letters I sent to your Mother/Grandmother and those she sent to me. Someday soon, when one of you is here, we'll give a reading session and see what two lovers, two hundred miles apart, had to say.

I wrote about the first three years of college in rather great detail. My recall of incidents was excellent. But now, as I look back to the time I left school at the end of my junior year to the marriage with your Mother/Grandmother, I remember very little. I can't even remember where I lived for my last semester, or any occurrences at school.

When I think of the store, I remember only that Dorothy Griffith was the bookkeeper, and Chubby McKee was our service man. We sold a lot of appliances: refrigerators, washers, dryers, and they all had to be serviced.

Of course, the times I went to Chicago to see your Mother/Grandmother and her visits to Taylorville are etched in my memory. I suppose the reason for my many lapses is that I was just marking time until my life would really begin...April 3, 1938.

Next chapter: the Wedding and the Honeymoon!  I could hardly wait!

MUCH LOVE -
Dad/GP

# My Life — Part 1
## The Wedding

In Yiddish "bubby" is a grandmother, and "mica" (soft c) is story. Thus, "bubbamica" is literally a grandmother story. In practice it becomes a story, usually from the past. This issue is a group of "bubbamicas," as they occur segmentally.

The wedding was lovely! Your M/GM planned it carefully with the help of Della Karlsson, my father's cousin. Della worked for a florist, and she had arranged wonderful bouquets for my bride and her bridesmaids... and also for the tables. Harry Johnson, Chicago's premier photographer, grabbed one of the bouquets for a picture. Della, who possessed the famous Rosenberg temper, screamed at him to leave her flowers alone. He did... and left immediately. That's why we have no pictures of the wedding.

Rabbi Herman Elliot Snyder came up from Springfield to officiate at the wedding. As he went through the ceremony, my knees began to tremble. As they knocked together, I worried that the sound would be distracting. But no one heard, as I was so frightened by this huge STEP in my life.

Another vignette: Francy, who was ten years old, was in charge of holding up the train of the fantastic gown worn by the bride. You all saw it at Tanya's wedding. Francy was too conscientious! In order to hold the train from getting on the floor, she pulled too hard and the bride had difficulty walking down the aisle.

We had a wonderful dinner... the Belmont Hotel was noted for its food... and there was lots of drinking. AND, there was lots of drinking! Carl Weinberger was the best man but he was the worst drinker. Lee took him home before eight o'clock. Babe, M/GM's brother, who adored his sister, celebrated her wedding a bit too much. He was taken to one of the rooms for a cold shower...with his clothes on!!!

These are the highlights of the wedding, as I remember them. One more comment about the drinking. M/GM made her father promise not to get drunk. She was quite pleased, because he didn't. My father was OK too. He didn't drink or smoke and he told everyone how rigid he was. I don't know if this is true or not, but someone said that, on the first night of their honeymoon, Dad told mother, "We'll have sex on Tuesdays, Thursdays, and Saturdays. Since this is Sunday, good night!"

## PART II - THE HONEYMOON

The wedding was on Sunday. That night we went to the bridal suite at the Drake Hotel. Neither of us got much sleep. We must have been nervous about the momentous event in our lives. Also, your M/GM was forgetful. Someone gave her a gorgeous nightgown for the first night and she left it at the Drake…I think it was in the original box.

I didn't plan the honeymoon very well…just to drive south, with possible stops in Memphis and New Orleans. We got a late start and when it got dark, we stopped at Effingham, a small town in Illinois, about fifty miles east at Taylorville.

The hotel was the only one in town, appropriately called the Effingham Hotel. This was Monday night and it was full of traveling men who were starting their week. There was no air conditioning and the transom was open for ventilation. This enabled us to hear the men across the hall better. They kept us awake all night as they played poker, and drank, and went to the only bathroom on the floor, which was down the hall. Not really an auspicious beginning.

The next day was better. We drove to Memphis, got a lovely room at a warm, wonderful southern hotel, the Peabody. We liked it so much that we stayed there for the rest of the honeymoon. I had told your M/GM not to take along any long dresses as we wouldn't need them. That was one of my first mistakes. The Peabody required suits and long dresses in the dining room two nights a week. We ate in the coffee shop those two nights; M/GM gently (?) reminded me of my error.

The highlight of our honeymoon was the night of "The Emperor." Let me explain. Your M/GM was so upset by this huge change in her life that she didn't have a B.M. for five days. No medication or prunes helped, so I went to the drug store and bought an enema bag. It was named THE EMPEROR. Of course, I couldn't be the nurse and do the insertion. It was too embarrassing for such a new relationship. So I did the next best thing. I coached from outside the closed bathroom door. Your M/GM, who had never seen an enema bag before, had an awful time. Ultimately, she managed, and everything came out right in the end.

We left for Taylorville on Friday. My father insisted that I be there for work on Saturday, because that was 'payday" for the coal mines that were the main source of income for the city of Taylorville. Your M/GM took rather strong exception to my father's demands. She went so far as to call him a dictator. They say the apple doesn't fall too far from the tree. But really, do I show any of those tendencies??

Next Chapter - The Honeymoon Cottage. I can hardly wait!

# A Tale of Two Houses on Park Street

## PART I - 708 W. PARK

The first house was 708 W. Park, which was our "honeymoon cottage."
Visualize a rectangular building, and then divide it in half the long way.
The front half, facing the street, was a long living room and a dinette. The
other half had a kitchen and two bedrooms with a bathroom in between.
It was a new idea that didn't work! It was built with cinder blocks instead
of concrete. The walls had a tendency to lean out at the top. Even though
heavy steel rods were used to pull the walls back, there were cracks that
permitted rain to enter without permission. We had buckets everywhere
to catch the pure rainwater. Excellent for shampoos!

But we were happy there. The rent was too high... $28.00 per month, but
we furnished it with "modern" furniture and enjoyed our early married
years tremendously. Our first three children were born there: Snowball,
Arlene, and Toto... in that order,

I was getting a haircut for fifty cents and the barber asked me if I wanted
a dog. Of course, I agreed. The next day, he brought us a gorgeous white
Spitz... which we promptly named "Snowball." She was fully grown but
young, and very smart. She'd walk the full length of the living room
on her hind legs at my urging...with a treat at the end of this remark-
able achievement. M/GM was crazy about her... they spent many hours
together.

I was happy with my job at the store. Bernie Kalis and I were the sales
force and I learned a lot from him. Unfortunately, 1938 was a recession
year, but business bounced back in 1939.

A huge problem came into our lives when M/GM had a "difference of opinion" with my father. My parents and Estelle and Francy lived at 311 E. Park, the second house in this story. We (i.e. M/GM and I) were expected to be at 311 E. Park promptly at noon every Sunday for a huge dinner. We liked to sleep late on Sunday mornings, and were generally late for this important weekly event.

One Sunday we were especially late and, at the dinner table, my father went on and on ad nauseam about the importance of being on time, how we hurt the timing of the cook (my mother) and how discourteous it was to keep the entire family waiting. Your M/GM, not the most patient person in the world, finally exploded. She yelled, "Daddy, shut up!!!"

There was a long period of absolute silence. No one, but no one, ever spoke to Louis H. Cohn that way and certainly not a 19-year-old kid. Very little was said for the rest of the meal.

The next day, Louis H. Cohn called me into his office and said, "Well, it looks like we can't get along, so you'll have to leave." I was crushed. Where could I go? What could I do? I don't recall what happened next, but I do remember "Zeyde" coming down from Chicago and having a long conference with my dad. A decision was reached that we would look for a store for me to operate.

We found a store for sale... but not for me. It was in Decatur, and my father had always wanted to live in a larger city. We bought the store and my dad moved to Decatur to run that store, leaving the Taylorville store for me.

I was delighted! My salary went from $35.00 per week to $65.00 per week.

Most importantly, this change gave me the opportunity to hone my skills in all phases of the operation... buying, advertising, collections, as well as sales. We were able to move into my parents' home also.

## PART II - 311 E. PARK STREET

Before we moved to 311 E. Park, we asked the landlady if she'd sell. Yes, she would, but she wanted $3,750.00. Forget it... no house is worth that much money.  So we paid the huge rent of $35.00 a month.

It was a wonderful house!  The downstairs had a kitchen, dining room, and living room; upstairs had two and a half bedrooms and a bathroom. When I lived there before I wed, I had the half-bedroom.  The yard was quite large and M/GM had a big vegetable garden in the backyard.

But I get ahead of my story.  Prior to moving into 311 E. Park, there were two momentous, explosive events that changed our lives completely: World War II was brewing and Arlene was born.

My mother and father were going to a B'nai Brith Convention and really wanted baby pictures of their first grandchild to take with them.  So, because Arlene was delaying her entrance (as usual), the four of us rode many bumpy country roads to induce her to forsake her womb like existence.  It worked... and they got their pictures of the most beautiful baby that was ever born up to that time.

We had two tragedies.  The first one involved breast feeding... the milk wouldn't come out properly, causing infection.  M/GM wound up in a hospital in Springfield with through and through drains in each breast. She finally healed, but it was very traumatic.

The second tragedy occurred when mother and child were coming home to 708 W. Park.  As we turned the corner one block from our house, we saw Snowball lying in the street.  She had just been hit by a car and killed. Our first child had died.  It was awful.

To partially heal our wounds, we got another Spitz and for some odd reason named her Toto.  She was a nice dog but she couldn't take the place of Snowball.  Her chief claim to fame in our memories was her propensity to jump in the baby carriage with Arlene when Arlene was napping in the yard.

I shall never forget December 7, 1941.  One of my closest friends, E Reisman was visiting us.  He had come from an army training camp in Missouri. We were having dinner.  Someone called and told us to turn on the radio. We did and got the dreadful news about Pearl Harbor.  E (for Ezra) turned white because he knew he would have a major involvement in the war. It definitely brought about a major change in my life also.

My right-hand-man was Wally Heil, and he had a friend, George Butler, who ran a welding school for the U.S. government. It was designed for men like Wally and me who were fathers, not subject to the draft, who were willing to help with the war effort. Wally persuaded me to enter this program with him and we both became accomplished welders.

I was hired by the Pullman Co. to help weld the Liberty ships they were building in Chicago. In June of 1942 we made our second move...7014 S. Crandon, Chicago, Illinois.

NEXT CHAPTER - THREE YEARS IN CHICAGO - IT WAS FUN!

# Chapter VII
# Chicago — 1942 - 1945

Before I tell you what happened in Chicago, I want to write about my father. He came off as "the heavy" in the last two chapters, which exhibited his rigidity and feelings of self-importance. Actually, he was a very kindly, loving man who probably had strong feelings of inferiority. I'll not analyze him, but I wanted all of you to know that he, like everyone else, had positive as well as negative attributes. He was very good to me and my family and we all loved him.

Now on to Chicago where, for the first time in my life, I lived in a large city. We had a lot of family there. Zeyde and Bess, Babe and Beverly, Donna and Jill, Aunt Lee and Harriet, Della and Mervin, Aunt Esther and Benny. We saw a lot of Zeyde and Bess as well as Babe and his family, who lived near us.

I was always a skinny kid (weighed 119 pounds when I graduated college) so the concept of my making a living doing "man's work" was quite gratifying. I was a good welder and rose to the exalted position of "Leader," or straw boss. Picture a Liberty ship (or any ship) and slice it as you would a loaf of bread. These "sections" were welded from top to bottom at the Pullman Co. in South Chicago. When completed, they were taken on flat cars by rail to the Pullman Co. dock on Lake Michigan. There the sections were welded together, and made into a complete ship. It was a great idea and quite fascinating.

I used my second name, Ralph, at work. This confused your M/GM who would hang up when one of my friends at work would call me.

Our apartment was very nice. We lived on the third floor which was quite high because we had to walk up to the first floor. It was a narrow, long building and each of the three apartments was the length of the building. We climbed a lot of stories to get there, but we were young and thought nothing of it.

174

We wanted another child, but your M/GM couldn't conceive because our doctor in Taylorville was negligent. But Dr. Ernes, whom M/GM adored, fixed her up and we got our wonderful Vicki. She had big blue eyes, almost bald, and said nothing for two years. She must have been observing us and her environment because once she started to talk, she didn't stop. When Grandma Glass visited us and saw that Vicki wasn't talking, she told me we should pay more attention to her. Old world wisdom!

I forgot to mention that my best friend, Carl Weinberger, his wife, Lee, and daughter, Judy, lived in Chicago. They lived far north and we lived far south, so we saw them infrequently. When Carl and Lee had twins on January 3rd, 1943, Carl came out so we could celebrate together. Of course, he and I got drunk at our house and we decided to go out and get some hot dogs. Picture the scene: icy streets, very cold weather, two drunken men and a pregnant woman (M/GM heavy with Vicki) going into a tavern on 71st Street ordering hot dogs. They threw us out!

Ten months after Vicki was born M/GM became pregnant with David. Zeyde was so upset because of the closeness of these two babies, he made Bess (his wife) talk to M/GM to make sure she know what causes pregnancy. We thought that was funny. Anyhow, David arrived just before the stroke of midnight December 31st, 1944. Now we had three beautiful children. David was quite fair, with curly blonde hair which he inherited from the Grandma he never saw. He was a good baby... he had to be... because M/GM had her hands full with two babies and a 4 ½-year-old daughter who resented her siblings a lot. At that time, your M/GM was a real "shtarker"– a very strong person. She did the laundry in the basement (almost four stories down) and took care of the large apartment and three children quite successfully. I must admit that I did very little - that was "women's work!!" How times have changed!!

All during the time we lived in Chicago, the big news was the WAR...which he followed avidly. Manpower became critical, so they began to draft young men with children. I got my draft notice and we made plans immediately for M/GM and the children while I'd be in the service. A decision was reached to move them to Decatur so that they'd be close to Boppa and Gommy. We bought a very nice Dutch Colonial, two-story house at

12 Lincoln Place, just across the street from Grandpa and Grandma who lived at 3 Lincoln Place. It was a lovely home.

I was lucky! The Army doctor who examined me didn't like the murmur in my heart and I was rejected. They gave me a 4F classification.

My father needed me in the Decatur store, the war was winding down, and we had already bought the house, so we moved to Decatur... our fourth home in our first seven years of marriage!

NEXT CHAPTER - DECATUR, THE EARLY YEARS

# Chapter VIII
# Decatur
# The Early Years

We were well ensconced in our home at 12 Lincoln Place and I was happy selling furniture and appliances again. Arlene was six years old and went to school at Mary W. French, a school from kindergarten through sixth grade, not too far from our home. Vicki and David also went there and had to compete with "Straight A Arlene."

The Decatur store was built for furniture and appliance sales. It was quite large with balconies for display as well as the first floor. The second floor was the warehouse.

Mr. Mains, an old Leath man from Danville had been the manager of the Taylorville store ever since I left. After the war, Wally Heil returned home and got his old job back selling furniture for Mr.. Mains in the Taylorville store. One day, I think it was early 1946, Wally came to Decatur to see me. He had a simple message: Mr. Mains was a lousy manager, and if I didn't get back there soon, the store would go belly-up.

I discussed this problem with my dad and gave him my solution to the problem: I'll buy the Taylorville store and pay him back out of the profits. He agreed with me and I got the opportunity of my lifetime - a chance to be on my own and become successful in business.

The timing was just right! During the war, furniture was limited and rationed. After the war there was a pent-up demand for everything. The men from the area had returned from war. There were four coal mines that worked full time and Christian County was booming. Taylorville was the county seat. Hewitville was a small village at the edge of town surrounding Peabody mine #58. Then there was the "midland" - Kincaid, Tovey, and Jellyville, where mines #7, #8, and #9 were located.

This move gave me the opportunity to spread my wings and fly as a highly successful entrepreneur. I made enough money in eight years to pay off my dad and open the second store in Decatur in 1954. We'll come to that venture in a subsequent chapter. I did so well that when my father decided to retire in 1950 and offered me the Decatur store, I turned him down. I was just doing too well in Taylorville and couldn't spread myself too thin.

I commuted those eight years from 12 Lincoln Place in Decatur to the store in Taylorville. Initially, I drove a pickup truck, because we couldn't afford a car.

As I look back now, I realize that I must have been delinquent as a father and husband. I worked long hours, the business was the center of my world, and I had little time for my family. In retrospect, I was the same when I had the Decatur store. I suppose everyone pays a price for success.

These were the growing years for AVD. They were all wonderful children and we did have quality time together. Gommy and Boppa lived across the street and we went to their home for many wonderful meals. Your M/GM was a good cook too, and we entertained frequently.

Two of our closest friends were the Appelbaums and Bachrachs. Together, we were the ABC Club and had parties together. One time, the three couples held a "surprise party." We invited a large number of couples to come to our home first. We served drinks in our basement, but no hors d'oeuvres. One person from the group cried, "Not even a cracker?"

Then, we all boarded a bus for an unknown destination. Irving Appelbaum, Henry Bachrach, and I "peddled" drinks and food up and down the aisles. Henry, a very small man, was placed on the rack over the seats by a group of men who were feeling no pain. We wound up in a restaurant in Pana for a chicken dinner. I was the chief planner of this event. I suppose this was my first opportunity to exhibit my penchant for "unusual parties." I love it!

What else do I remember about 12 Lincoln Place? Well, there was the time I came home from work and was greeted with the news that David and his boyfriend Jimmy were jumping from the roof of the house to the roof of the garage - about three or three and a half feet. Of course, I was furious. He could have killed himself and we'd have lost all the money we invested in him. I think that was the only time I beat him.

Then there was the time that M/GM and I were quarreling. That sweet little old lady had a hellava temper. She was so furious that she threw a large bowl of freshly made chopped liver at me. I was quick on my feet, dodged, and the bowl broke and spilled all over the dining room floor. When M/GM flew out of the house in a rage, AVD began to cry. I placated them immediately, "Don't worry kids. She won't leave us. I have the keys to her car."

Another memory was the patio that never got built. We had saved $1,000 for that patio, but gave it to the U.J.A. when Israel became a state in 1984. That was a lot of money then - about $20,000 - $25,000 in today's inflated currency. Honestly, we never regretted it.

Another incident involved Dr. Beyda. It seemed that, many times that M/GM ate and drank at a party, she would wake up in the middle of the night feeling cold and clammy, with diarrhea and a strong desire to vomit. Dr. Beyda said to call him at any time and he'd come over. I did. It was 4:00 a.m. and he didn't arrive until 5:00, all shaved and dressed in a suit and tie. By then she felt better. When we moved to Sarasota, our doctor, Larry Phillips, diagnosed her problem: it is IHSS (Idiopathic Hypertrophic Subaortic Stenosis). She still takes a beta blocker regularly and it works. The problem is a muscle growth in her left ventricle which impedes the flow of blood to the aorta.

Two major events occurred in our lives in 1953. I started planning the Decatur store and we moved to 777 S. Monroe. I'll talk about the store in the next chapter, but I'll recount now the events leading up to the purchase of the new house and its importance in our lives.

As you know, your M/GM has large eyes. However, when I came home from the Taylorville store one evening, her eyes were as big as saucers...

and luminous. "What happened?" I asked. She replied, "I've seen our new home!" It seems that my dad had taken her to see the empty house at 777 S. Monroe... it was for sale... and she wanted it. They took me over to see it and I wanted it too. What was not to like? It was a regal brick English mansion with slate roof and copper gutters sitting in the middle of one and three-quarter acres of beautifully landscaped ground. A city park was on one side and the land rolled down to the road that adjoined the Sangamon River.

We bought it and promptly engaged a designer friend of my sister, Estelle, (Bill something) to work over the interior and get it furnished with really nice furniture...not what I sold. Your M/GM loved that house so much that, twenty-four years later, I had a hard time getting her to move to Sarasota.

NEXT, CHAPTER IX - SUCCESS IN BUSINESS AND LIFE IN DECATUR

# Chapter IX
# Success in Business
# & Life in Decatur

## PART I - THE FURNITURE STORE

I am now about to condense twenty-four years of furniture business in Decatur into a few pages. How time can fly! In the last chapter, I wrote that I couldn't buy my dad's store in Decatur in 1950 because I was too involved with the Taylorville store and that venture was so successful because of my participation. But it was logical to have a store in Decatur because we lived there. I couldn't drive back and forth to Taylorville forever and we didn't want to live there.

Early in 1953 my entrepreneurial blood began to boil when I spotted an empty building on the corner of Broadway and North. It had been a foundry, and there was a lot between it and the next building (Campbell's Auto Supply) which belonged to the same owner as the foundry. I bought that old building, the lot next to it, and a parking lot of the other side of Campbell's subject to our ability to work out the plans for the store.

You see, the foundry was not large and the lot next door was only twenty feet. If we built a two story building on the lot, we'd have a little over seven thousand square feet of floor space... quite small for a furniture store.

We did it! My good friend, contractor Walter Ware, had plans drawn up and we signed a contract for the building in July of 1953 at Francy and Buddy Melnik's house. The temperature was noted at the top of the contract... 113°.

I had to plan carefully because the store was so small. I rented a large warehouse a few blocks away so we could have sample goods at the store and a lot of "backup" in the warehouse. That plan worked and we opened in the fall of 1954 with instant success.

Much of our sales were in living room furniture. Our main supplier, Kroehler Co. had just come out with bumper and two piece sectionals. Bumper means no arms on each end. The public liked them, and other items we stocked, so we made money immediately. A new broom sweeps clean, and we were the new kid on the block.

There were two ladies in the office. Carl Besalke and Walt Fitzgerald were my salesmen. Bud Fansler was the warehouse manager. We also had four delivery and warehouse personnel. Those early years were the halcyon days.

I must admit that I was passionate about my store. I worked long hours as sales manager, office manager, buyer, and advertising manager. And yes, I worked on collections, too. Many times I wrote the weekly ad on Sunday because I didn't have time during the week. But - I loved it!

As I look back now, I spent most of my life for the next twenty-four years in that little building. We found our niche in Decatur as one of the many "time payment" houses with a large accounts receivable and many loyal customers. Some of those people still come in and call Roger "Mr. Cohn" and ask how his dad is doing. I'm proud to say that every year was profitable.

In 1974 I had a small heart attack. I lost 10% of my heart and my great interest in the furniture business. M/GM bought a cute little townhouse in Sarasota, to make me get out of the store occasionally and the thought of retirement became more and more appealing. But, how do you sell a furniture store? With big investment in inventory, property, and accounts receivable, it would be difficult. So I devised a plan: to hire a manager and then sell to him.

I had heard about the manager of Leath Furniture Co., a chain store operating in the Midwest. Those who knew him said he was a nice guy and very capable. I thought that Roger Rosenkranz might be the right man for my plan. After I met him, I knew he was. In fact, his plan was the same as mine! He wanted to manage Cohn Furniture for five years and then buy it... paying for it out of the profits.

He left our meeting saying he'd talk it over with Ollie, his wife, and get back to me. A week went by and no call from Roger. Finally, I called him and he said that they decided not to do it. "Why not?" I asked. "Because of you and your bad heart," he replied. I laughed and laughed then. "You come on down," I said, "I'm going to live a long time." He did and we made the deal exactly as outlined above. He was to pay dollar for dollar for all inventories, accounts receivable, and real estate when he took over... but no "good will."

Meanwhile, M/GM and I were spending more and more time in our townhouse. I didn't mention the first fire in 1963... forty years ago... which destroyed the building. It started with a spark from a faulty electrical connection. The store was rebuilt exactly as it had been, and we operated out of the warehouse... now just one block east. We were selling furniture there when Kennedy was shot.

Now we come to the second fire, which was in 1977, almost fourteen years later. We found out later that it was set by thieves to cover up their theft of a lot of merchandise. M/GM and I were awakened early one morning in Sarasota with the bad news.

I got plane tickets immediately to return home, and then took Barbie (our beautiful collie) out to a kennel on Cattlemen Road. I got gas at B'hai Vista and Beneva and I was so concerned I told the attendant the whole story about the fire and how sad it would be to go back. As I left, he cheerfully said, "Have a good day!"

This fire was complete devastation, so we rebuilt a much larger store with a second story over the entire building.

After Roger was on his own for a while, he bought the Campbell Auto Supply next door and made it into a chain store. He has fulfilled all my expectations, made a lot of money for himself, and has maintained our tradition: this year will be the 49th year of profitable operation on that corner where I spotted that old former foundry.

The Taylorville store had a disastrous ending. It was a separate corporation, and all I ever received from it, after I left in 1954, was a small monthly check as President. I foolishly left the entire operation up to Wally Heil, who was a good salesman but a poor manager. Of course, we bought the same inventory and planned the same events, but years and years went by on a virtual "break-even" basis. I'm an old softie and I felt an obligation to Wally, who had helped me so much in the eight years I ran the Taylorville store.

I don't remember the year, but I was in my seventies when I left Sarasota to go to Taylorville to help Wally with our "Going Out of Business" sale. I really enjoyed it... back in the saddle again... that was the last time I sold furniture.

Ethel Feser was the bookkeeper and she was also Wally's lover. When I asked her for a final accounting, she stalled and stalled. When she committed suicide, we knew something was wrong. It turned out that she had "cooked the books" for years so that Wally could maintain his position. Even after the store building and warehouse were sold, there was little left for AVD. I had given them all the stock.

You win some... and you lose some! I'll never forget the sign that hung in my dad's office in the Taylorville store. It read "Nothing is as bad as you think it is and nothing is as good as you think it is." We all make mistakes (such as my confidence in Wally Hail) and we all do good things. Life is made up of pluses and minuses. When you add up the sum and there are more pluses than minuses, you're a WINNER!

NEXT, CHAPTER X - SUCCESS IN REAL ESTATE IN DECATUR

# Chapter X — Success in Real Estate in Decatur

My father, Louis H. Cohn, died in 1965. He was almost 73 years old. At the time, that was considered a long life. What a change in longevity in one generation! Most of estate was in income real estate. I handled it all for thirty years. My mother had all the funds she needed and the corpus was the same when she died in 1994.

Within a year after I took over, we had a problem. The city of Decatur was buying properties, and the piece we rented to Hertz Rent-All was one of them. They rented all kinds of thing: tools, wheel barrows, etc.

I mentioned this to my dentist, Dr. John Baxley, who was a better builder than a dentist. "Not to worry, Gersh," he said. "Buy a lot and I'll have my T&T Builders erect a building for you." I did and they did. We had a nice building on Eldorado Street at a nominal price.

This was the building that became Trust #400. I realized that my mother would have sufficient income without it, so I had her gift it to all her children, their spouses, and grandchildren. I made distribution for many years until Hertz went out of business. Then, we sold the building and distributions were made until the new owners paid it off.

It was about this time that Ken Huston, a big shot real estate promoter and developer moved back to Decatur. He loved partnerships and he set about getting me into one with him. "Let's rent that three acres on North Main Street. The lease is cheap and we'll move out the trailers some day and build some commercial building," was his pitch. He needed me for the credit to handle the financing. "I'll do all the work and handle everything," was his promise. I was intrigued and we did it. More about this later.

One day Ken came to me with an idea. He wanted me to buy three lots on Eldorado Street to develop. He promised to get a tenant for whom I'd build a building for income. I said, "No." He then said, "Would you buy them with your friend, John Baxley, if he'd do it?" I said, "Yes" and promptly forgot about it.

A month or two later, there was a knock on our door at 9:00 p.m. It was Ken Huston, "Congratulations!" he said, "You and Doc just bought the three lots on Eldorado Street!"

# Chapter XI
# Lincoln Manor

It was late in the year of 1968. I was on the floor at the store waiting for the next victim... I mean customer... when Ray Carmine walked in. Ray was a good friend, a real estate man, and a buddy in "Toastmasters," a self-help group.

"What brings you here?" I asked. "Oh," he replied, "I came here to sell you a building." He then explained that he had a large home on two acres of ground, just a few blocks from downtown. "What in the world would I want that for?" I asked. Quick as a flash, he said, "For a shelter care residence."

My interest was aroused immediately, as I had heard a long discussion of shelter care the previous week. I was having lunch with my good friend John Baxley, who had researched shelter care in depth because he had a piece of ground in the west end that he wanted to sell to some people. He thought it would be good for shelter care. He explained how it would work and that it would be a great investment.

When Ray showed me the property, I was excited. The price was right... only $50,000 and the two acres were long and narrow... ideal for two wings. The house would be incorporated into the shelter care facility. I put down a deposit of $5,000 to hold the property until I could finalize plans.

When I shopped the Furniture Mart in Chicago, I always visited my best friend, Carl Weinberger. He was then manufacturing furniture... The Cambridge Co. He knew of my modest success in real estate in Decatur and asked me to let him invest in my next venture. I thought that it would be great to have him, Buddy Melnik, my brother-in-law and good friend, and Seymour Chazin, in this shelter care investment. Seymour was Carl's friend who became my accountant and very good friend also. My three best friends and I could have a lot of fun and make money, too.

They all agreed that it was a great opportunity and we decided to do it. Carl and Seymour had strong statements and, with mine, we could borrow the money we needed for the structure. Buddy knew about building and air conditioning and he could help me run the home. We made a huge mistake: we brought in Bob Packer, a so-called "professional" because we knew nothing about the business. He was the administrator for Lakeshore Manor, a nursing home owned by his father-in-law and brother-in-law. More about his ineptness later.

The financial structure was simple: five equal partners. Carl and Seymour would put up $20,000 each and Bob, Buddy, and I just $10,000 each. The other $10,000 on our part came from our services in the building and start-up phase. Since we started operation early in 1969, there was a large income tax deduction because of our early losses. It was decided that we become a sub-chapter S corporation for business purposes.

Buddy had a friend who was an engineer. He did all the layout work, which he had an architect friend sign. The west wing joined the house with parking adjacent to this wing. We took advantage of the sloping ground and built a two-story wing on the east, which also was joined to the large home. The latter had some rooms as well as offices.

Now, I want to digress for a moment. Henry Bachrach and I had been buying stock in a furniture manufacturing company called "Dolly Madison." I bought odd chests and beds from this firm and the salesman got me involved with the stock. The price gyrated tremendously and Henry and I never did know when to sell.

At that point, I had a huge dilemma. My greedy side said, "Look, Dolly Madison is worth $150,000 now. Why not sell it and use the money to finance Lincoln Manor, the name I'd chosen for the shelter care facility. This is going to be a wonderful investment and it's your deal. Why give it away? You don't need partners. Your credit and the $150,000 is enough. Besides, you can hire professionals to lay it out and take care of the day-to-day management."

These arguments ran through my head for several days, until I finally turned to the "greedy me" and said, "You have some good points, but I gave my word and that's worth all the money in the world." And that settled the argument. It was ironic, though, that I ultimately sold Dolly Madison stock for a pittance.

Subsequently, Buddy came to me at a restaurant where I was having lunch. "Do you mind if I sell half of my share to Mort?" he asked. "Yes, I do," I replied. "Well, it's too late. I did it." Buddy had borrowed the $10,000 that he had to put up and, by selling to Mort, he got in for nothing and that's how we got Mort, who borrowed the money from his father-in-law.

Gabe Wolff came in because Seymour told me they were partners in their investments, as well as their accounting practice. The only good thing that our so-called "professional" did for us was to recommend that we hire Mary Miller as our administrator. That was OK but Mary was my book-keeper and I had to hire another one... Geraldine Griffith. Parenthetically, Gerry is 90 years old now and I hear from both her and Mary Miller occasionally.

Well, we opened Lincoln Manor in August 1970. It was well-received and Mary had it filled within three months.

At the Grand Opening, the major discussion was "bathrooms." I got the sense that (1) people really wanted private bathrooms (We had one for four people) and (2) older people have two major concerns: what goes in their mouth and what comes out of their rectum.

I immediately conceived the idea of a residence for private pay... no state aid... with a bathroom adjoining every room. I went to see an architect, Harry Caldwell, who had just what I wanted... drawings for another client in a different city... a quadrangular building for ninety residents which could be a "flop-over" for another ninety residents. The first part became Lincoln Manor, North.

In April of 1971, Buddy, Mort, and I bought the stock of Bob Packer. I got 10% more shares and they each got an additional 5%. Bob was happy... he made $10,000 and didn't do anything but tell jokes to Mary Miller. Mort ultimately sold that 5% to his brother, Seymour, and Seymour later acquired 7 ½%, or half of Buddy's stock in some kind of family deal. He's the only one with real money in the venture and he's getting his money's worth. To complete the story of the stock transfers... bit by bit, I distributed 8% to Arlene, Vicki, and David. Carl gave some of his to his children also.

Mary Miller was our administrator for seven years. Then a squabble ensued regarding Buddy's wish to have our prescriptions filled at the pharmacy of his choice. When she left, Tom Booth took her place for eight years. At that time, we sold Lincoln Manor, South (the original) for $15,000 per bed. Since the mortgage had been paid, this large sum was all profit.

We were left with Lincoln Manor, North which was under the guidance of Shelba Donoho, another employee of mine. LMN was started in 1973 (the phone # is 875-1973) and completed in 1975. It was not very profitable, as the original ninety beds were not the quantity for a successful operation. When we added two wings... instead of the flopover ninety as originally planned... each with twenty-five beds, all was well. All that took place during the tenure of Shelba, which lasted twelve years. We had great success with "private pay" at LMN and we still have a high percentage of P.P. I just remembered that I failed to state that not long after we opened LMS, the state of Illinois eliminated "shelter care" status and we have been intermediate nursing ever since. In fact, one wing of LM is now a twenty-five bed "skilled care" facility.

After serving us well for twelve years, Shelba Donoho felt that she was "burned out." Her husband, Terry, also wanted his wife back. The position of nursing home administrator is a very demanding one. Not only is there a lot of responsibility, but it is also quite time consuming. It reminds me of the old adage "Mother's work is never done," and the administrator is mother to one hundred forty residents and all the employees.

When Shelba told me she was going to retire, I had an immediate thought about her replacement - Sheila McClung. Sheila came to Lincoln Manor South as an aid. This is the one who wipes bottoms and cleans up vomit. She was ambitious, went to nursing school, and because a nurse. She worked her way up as an assistant to Tom Booth. When I called her, she said, "Mr.. Cohn, you called at just the right time. I've passed my boards for administrator and I'm leaving LMS to get another job.

In Yiddish, there's a word "Besheart" which means that it was "meant to be." Finding Sheila in 1987 to be our administrator was our lucky day. She has done a magnificent job and our hope is that she doesn't get too much "burnout"... and that she keeps working for many years.

As for me, I was the CEO of both units for twenty-five years. As a senior "senior citizen," I retired to the easy job of Chairman of the Board, and Seymour Melnik has done an admirable job as President ever since.

Have I ever regretted taking partners? Never! Lincoln Manor has been one of the joys of my life and it has been a pleasure to have shared it with such wonderful people... who have contributed, each in his (or her) way, to our success. The combined wisdom of many bright and interesting people has given us great impetus.

As I look back over the thirty-three years of Lincoln Manor's existence, I see a lot more than great financial success. I see a lot of love on the part of many people. I see the love of a Board of Directors who voted unanimously when L.M. was in its infancy... to put the needs and comfort of the residents first and foremost. And- they have maintained that value all through the years.

Then there is the love of the Family Council which has met regularly to work with our key employees for the betterment of L.M. Above all is the love of our employees whose work has enabled our frail elderly to enjoy their final years. Two prime examples - (1) Arlene Waller, Activity Director at LMN for twenty-eight years. She loved her work and she loved the residents and (2) Sheila McLung, our Administrator, for the past sixteen years, whose energy, dedication, and love of the residents have made a huge contribution to our success.

As I look at Lincoln Manor with perspective I see a well-respected, important institution in the Decatur community. I am proud to say that I am the founder of that wonderful institution.
MUCH LOVE,
    ❏ Dad    ❏ G.P.

This is the old house that became the cornerstone for Lincoln Manor. It was built before the Civil War and Abraham Lincoln visited here. Thus the name: LINCOLN MANOR.

# Chapter XII - My Life Decatur — Jews, Wasps, & Blacks

When I wrote about my early life growing up in small towns in Illinois, I pointed out my acceptance of second class citizenship as a Jew. Nothing overt... just acceptance of the #1 position of Wasps, with Jews and Blacks in a secondary role.

Decatur was a larger version of those towns. The Decatur Club... mostly for dining... and the Decatur Country Club had the same old restrictions: no Jews or Blacks allowed!

The Black people lived in a segregated area, as they still do in Sarasota and most cities, and mixing with them was frowned upon. A case in point was an incident in 1959 or 1960. I was called by my friend, a sergeant at the police station, to come down and get my daughter, Vicki. She had committed the unpardonable sin: she and her girlfriend were walking on some railroad tracks with two black boys. Nearby residents called the police and all four were taken to the police station. Things were quite different two generations ago.

Vicki was a good student and very popular with her siblings and teachers. It was only natural that she was chosen as an Exchange Student to go to a foreign country for the summer months. The selection committee met when they heard the news about Vicki's indiscretions and rescinded their selection. I insisted on speaking to them. They heard me but they didn't hear me. She was a bad, bad, girl!

Your M/GM and I have always felt strongly about racial and religious prejudice. And these feelings have been passed on to AVD. I was Chairman of the Decatur Human Relations Committee for two terms, and served on the Illinois Governor's Commission on Human Relations.

When I was Chairman in Decatur, I was harassed by the Chairman of the NAACP, James Gude. He came to every meeting and was highly critical, because things weren't moving fast enough. He frightened me with his deep, booming voice and scowling mien. However, we wound up as close friends and visited each other socially with Jerry Lesells, a man who worked with Jim at Staley's. Jim now lives in Ocala and we call each other occasionally.

The Jewish community had a goodly number of lawyers, doctors, one dentist, and a few scientists at Staley's. Oh, yes, one professor at Milliken. But by and large, we were shopkeepers. At one time there were four Jewish furniture stores, six or seven men's stores, and others in ladies' ready-to-wear, restaurants, tailors, etc. There were 100 to 125 families and much of our social life revolved around the Temple. Every Jew was a member, with dues from zero on up. My father and I were Presidents at the old Temple, and David was the first Bar Mitzvah at the new Temple. And there your M/GM held her bridge games and ran the gift shop. She made enough money with both enterprises to pay off the Rabbi's house and the Temple itself.

We were a group of 400 to 500 people who genuinely liked one another and got along together quite well. But - I don't want to give the impression that we lived segregated lives. Many of us were members of all kinds of civic groups, luncheon clubs, fraternal orders, and charitable organizations.

As I mentioned above, your M/GM and I were very close to the Gudes and Lesells, and we were the only Jews in a monthly pot luck bridge club.

There has been marked improvement in the black community in the past 50 years. The glass ceiling has been lifted in many corporations and government agencies, and education of the Wasps has helped alleviate some of the problems. Unfortunately, too many people look down on black people and delegate them to what I'll call "second class citizenship." Much more must be done.

Yes, there is still anti-Semitism and, in all probability, there always well be. But I honestly believe that we are now first class citizens and can hold up our heads with pride as we revel in the wonderful accomplishments of less than one half of one percent of the population of the world.

MUCH LOVE,

❏ Dad   ❏ GP   ❏ GGP

# Chapter XIII - Fond Memories of Decatur

We lived in Decatur for thirty-three years. I have written about my business ventures and activities and some of the memorable occurrences. Now, I want to tell you some of the memories I have that bring a smile to my face.

The first things I think about are my children, AVD, who lived a large part of their lives in Decatur. They went through grade school, high school, and college while living in Decatur and they all have fond memories of their lives there. I think of those activities that were important.

The first was breakfast... which I made while M/GM slept. The four of us enjoyed them. Then came the wild ride to school in my 300 H.P. Buick Rivera. VROOM! VROOM! VROOM! Everyone get out of the way.

Then there are the "Cohn Family Meetings." Arlene was the secretary and M/GM was generally the renegade who needed punishment. We decided, because of some indiscretion on her part, that she should have another child. This produced the Russian Veto. Another punishment was for M/GM to get up early and make breakfast. P.S. She still hates to get up in the morning and I still fix breakfast.

Getting back to the Cohn Family Meetings... David had a hard time being heard. The other four were loud and eloquent. So, he would turn to the wall and, in a low voice, have a conversation with an imaginary person. It was very funny at the time... also his famous observation that "coffee takes out all stains."

In retrospect, your M/GM and I didn't give AVD enough "quality time." I was engrossed in my business affairs and M/GM was too involved with organizations and running the bridge club and the Gift Shop at the Temple. Dr. Spock and others hadn't surfaced yet to let us learn the error of our ways. But, they all grew up in Decatur with strong family ties. They brought their "loves" home to meet us. Arlene was married in Chicago at

196

Aunt Estelle's home. It was quite fancy... it was catered by Gapers. And we had one down, two to go.

Vicki and Robert were married at our home. The wedding was quite lovely... on the first terrace in the back yard. Then we had a big party at the Hotel Orlando; lots of booze and dancing. Robert's parents, Geoffrey and Hazel, delighted the crowd with their "British Two Step."

Of course, M/GM and I had the wonderful experience of "Grand-parenting" as both Arlene and Vicki got into production early. We loved the visits that brought Sarah, Loren, Tanya, and Justin to Decatur. I remember the pool we erected above ground in our back yard and how much the kids loved it. (Parenthetically, I recall David swimming as a member of the Y team and how proud we were of him. I also recall going to the Y with Bill Lawler for relaxing steam baths and a rubdown.)

This story must be in print for posterity: Tanya visited us at Christmas (she was about four yours old). She came downstairs with the holiday wrapping and ribbons. Her grandma was in the kitchen at the sink. Behind her (almost touching) was a large man fixing our stove. "What are you going to do with those papers and ribbons? " GM said to Tanya. "I'm going to take them home with me." GM: "But what if your mommy and daddy won't let you?" Tanya: "They better, or I'll beat the shit out of them!" With that the large repairman started to shake as he tried to repress his laughter. Tanya has always had a way with words.

I spoke of Sylvia's interest in worthwhile organizations above. One of them, the League of Women Voters, gave her an afternoon she'll never forget. The speaker was Eleanor Roosevelt. Not only did Mrs.. Roosevelt give a wonderful speech, she had to go to Champaign for another meeting. This allowed M/GM as the President of the L of WV, the opportunity to drive her to Champaign. She'll never forget her afternoon with one of the greatest women of the 20th century.

What else do I remember? Well, we had fantastic holiday parties at our home in late December. The dining room table was a huge buffet with all kinds of delicacies. People would go round the table, and then go into the living room and den which had wall-to-wall people eating and drinking and talking. When the children of our friends went to college they became eligible to attend.

At this point, I'm recalling things at random. The ABC Club, Appelbaums, Bachrachs, and Cohns grew into an investment club. We added Francy and Buddy, Al and Shaan Schaar, Speedy and Mary Friedman, and Hans and Millie Wolff. We met once a month for a potluck dinner, as we all took turns as host and hostess. The latter furnished the meat course and the booze, while the rest brought everything else. We ate and drank to excess because everything was so good and then we wound up with lousy investments.

I suppose it's fair to say that our greatest coup d'état was having the famous Chicago Symphony String Quartet play a concert at our home. It all began when your M/GM saw an announcement in the Herald-Review that the Chicago Symphony was going to be in residence for a week in Decatur and that different units of the orchestra would be playing at the homes of local residents. It also advised that those interested should apply. Without wasting a moment, your M/GM wrote and requested one of their units for our home. Since she was the first to apply, she had her choice and she chose the quartet.

We invited thirty-two of our friends whom we felt would enjoy this type of music. Everyone came in their Sunday best and sat down in our living room. Then the quartet came in: the first and second violinists, the first viola, and the first cello of the world-famous orchestra. I remember only two names: Aitai, the leader and first violin and Miller, a marvelous cellist.

As they came in with their formal outfits, your M/GM and I greeted them in the hall. "What would you like us to play?" Aitai asked. Your M/GM was perplexed and said, "What would you like to play?" At this point Aitai whipped out a program that they played at a concert the week before. "That'll be fine," we said and they did it and it was absolutely marvelous.

I'm going to conclude with the animals, but I assure you, it'll be a long conclusion. First the dogs... I remember Sam, Teddy, Raffles, and Barbie. Sam was a large cocker spaniel, very sweet and very loving. His claim to fame came when he saw Ping, our first cat lying on the floor of the garage as a car was driving in. He dashed out, grabbed her by the neck and carried her out of the path of the car.

Vicki won Raffles in a raffle. Your M/GM and I told her we couldn't have another animal, as we had Teddy then and several cats. "Please, Daddy?" she begged, "let me go see it anyhow." We did and Vicki came out smiling. She had put Raffles, a very small puppy into her coat pocket. We relented and let her keep him, but nobody really liked Raffles. She looked like a fat, black hot dog with very short legs. M/GM liked her least because she insisted on going in the car with her, then insisted on sitting in her lap, and then sat there farting in her face. I think Vicki is the only one who loved her. She must have felt this antipathy because one day she left with the mailman and never returned.

Teddy, on the other hand, was loved by all of us. He was a large dog, a mixture of collie and German shepherd. He was quite loving, but he had a mean streak. We found out later that he was the dog who mauled a child on the East side of town. The child wanted to pet him while he was mating. He did not like children. Dr. Hubbell's little girl tried to pet him and he attacked her... almost got one eye. Dr. Hubbell insisted that I put him down and he was right. I had him put to sleep but I told M/GM that I gave him to a farmer. I told her the truth just a few years ago. He was really a Jekyll and Hyde dog but we all loved him.

Then we got Barbie, the most beautiful collie that ever lived. And she was smart, too. She was dog napped once and got away in two days. We were at Franny and Buddy's home one night and got a call from the Main Street Bar when she wandered in. They wouldn't serve her, so we went down and got her. We had a room for her beneath the end of the garage, but she wouldn't sleep there. On nights that were zero degrees, she'd relax on the snow. One of the funniest things I ever saw was when I looked out the breakfast room window and saw, emerging from "Barbie's Bedroom" (the room in the garage) about 8 or 9 of the most nondescript dogs you can imagine.

My fondest memory of Barbie in Decatur is when she'd meet me when I came home from work. She knew the time for me to come home. She'd sit and wait on our neighbor's yard two houses down from us at the curve in the road. When she saw me she'd get up and race me down the long driveway. And then greet me lovingly as if I'd been gone for a year or two. She was my dog!!

And now for the cats. Our first cat was Ping, a gorgeous Siamese cat with a vindictive temper. When she became pissed, she would piss...in the corner of the dining room, next to the bathroom. Cat urine is truly potent. Ping's urine went through the carpet and into the wood floor. David and I visited the old homestead two years ago and a faint aroma of Ping's rage was still there.

Then there was Herbie, another Siamese, who was so loving. He would crawl up onto M/GM's lap to bury his head in her neck. It was a great sight. Herbie was run over by a car when he wandered down to the drive at the bottom of our property. The young lad who did it wandered the neighborhood until he found us to return our wounded cat. We took Herbie to our vet who kept him at the kennel for a long time. His two back legs were crushed. This veterinarian did a wondrous job. He'd walk Herbie every day for a long time with a rope under his hindquarters. Herbie healed ultimately and was able to walk because of the heroic efforts of our vet. This story was told in our local newspaper and the A.P. picked it up. It was printed in numerous papers throughout the country, as we received copies from friends in diverse cities.

I wrote before about our cat Donna. She was named after Don Andrews, the man I went out to, to repossess all his furniture. A record player was missing so I took Donna, another gorgeous Siamese cat instead. Donna was living with us when Herbie had his accident. When she became pregnant, we were certain that she got out and met a gray-striped cat someplace. Herbie couldn't be the father... his rear end was crushed in his accident. When Jean and Wayne Gray and M/GM and I came home one Sunday from a bridge tournament, we found a group of little kittens... all SIAMESE! Herbie was still potent!

The amazing story about Donna and her kittens began when Vicki discovered five kittens on her bed. Donna had taken each kitten by the scruff of its neck and carried it from the basement up two flights of stairs and then on to Vicki's bed. When we took the kittens back to their bed in the basement, Donna did it again.

The last cat story is about Nudgie. She and Donna were the cats we brought to Sarasota. They're on our wall of pictures. This is the one where they're sitting with their backs together. I call this my "Siamese-Siamese cats."

Your M/GM had gone to Mayo Clinic in Minnesota to be with her brother Sam, who had an operation. I don't remember why I went there, but I was in a pet shop and saw this stunning six-month-old Siamese cat. I had to have it, so I bought it for a present for M/GM. When I broke down and told her what I'd done (when I called her in Minnesota) she was pleased. I told her she could name her anything she wanted when she returned, but I called her "Nudgie." This was because she had a "nudging" tone to her meow. Just then Nudgie shrilled "MEOWWW" in a harsh stentorian sound. Your M/GM said, "That's her name. She earns it."

We had other cats but these were the most interesting. They didn't call 777 S. Monroe "Cohn's Cathouse" for nothing. We had the finest pussies in the world!!!!

# Chapter XIV
# Sarasota
# The Early Days

Our first visit to Sarasota came after we had vacationed at Marco Island. This lovely island is about three hours south of Sarasota and, at that time, was a small retirement area for fishermen. We stayed at a lovely cottage owned by my sister, Estelle, and her first husband, Joe. I must tell you that Joe Mayer was a great guy. Estelle has been doubly blessed with two wonderful husbands.

We had driven down and went to Sarasota on the way back to visit our old friends, John and Norma Baxley. As we entered the city from the south, we saw a sign at Walt's Oyster Bar "OYSTERS - BAKER'S DOZEN - $1.00." I have always remembered that as a comparison point for today's inflated prices. We had a nice time with the Baxleys and were quite impressed with Sarasota.

Sequentially: 1. John Baxley sent me a brochure of "Summer Lake," his development of small, inexpensive town houses, which I promptly threw into the waste basket. 2. I had a small heart attack in 1974 (I was 58 years old). 3. John Baxley came back to Decatur on business. When he saw us, he showed your M/GM the brochure of Summer Lakes and told her this was the only way to get me out of the store. She said, "I'll do it!! I want that one in the corner." John was embarrassed. "Sylvia," he said, "that's the only one I've sold." She settled for the next one, and we were Florida-bound.

This townhouse was really nice. It was two stories, with two bedrooms and a bathroom on the second floor. The first floor had a living room, dinette area and kitchen. It wasn't large. Everything was small and compact. I had arranged to buy furniture at a wholesale house in Tampa. So, while Sylvia stayed with Norma, John and I went to Tampa in his truck and brought back light, colorful, Florida-style furniture to fill up the house.

202

It really looked good.

Summer Lakes is a self-contained unit, but the location wasn't great. The airport was a mile or two north and a mile south was "Newtown," an area confined to the black residents of Sarasota.

This location led to a big fight between your M/GM and Teedy Appelbaum, who had visited us. Teedy told someone that she was shocked to find the Cohns living in such a neighborhood. This got back to your M/GM and she was incensed...didn't speak to Teedy for a year or two. Then after Yom Kippur services, your M/GM went over to Teedy at the Temple, put her arm around her, and said, "I forgive you." They have been best friends ever since.

We always drove to Sarasota, bringing Barbie, Donna, and Nudgie with us. One Thanksgiving, your M/GM baked two cakes and left them on the dinette table and we went to the Slosbergs for Thanksgiving dinner. When we returned, we ran into big, big trouble. Barbie had eaten the two cakes, then vomited and pooped all over the dinette area. We turned as green as the carpet and spent hours cleaning up the mess. Barbie learned a great lesson: she couldn't have her cake and eat it too!

We had wonderful visits from our children and grandchildren. One time Tanya came by plane from Baltimore. I can picture her now walking down from the plane to the ground. She was so small and pretty and so alone.

Then there was the memorable time that Arlene called me and said, "Daddy, can we (Loren, Sarah, and her) come down for a week?" I reminded her about the five day maximum that the old curmudgeon had set up. She called back again. "Daddy, the special rate on the plane is for a week." Of course, I relented and we all had a great week together. As they left, Arlene said, "Daddy, the week was OK, wasn't it?" I replied, "It was wonderful, but five days would have been better."

We would come to Sarasota intermittently...for a week, two weeks, or a month. The big turning point came in the spring of 1977. Bob and Harriette Hirsh were visiting us and I took them (and M/GM) on a tour of my favorite area in Sarasota, Bird Key. I pulled over at the corner of Spoonbill and Blue Jay Place and pointed to the vacant lot. "I bought that lot today." Well, your M/GM went ballistic! She loved her home at 777 S. Monroe, Decatur, Illinois, and wasn't about to move. I lied, of course, "not to worry... it's just a good investment."

I have always been a "control person" (please, not a "control freak") and I will probably always be one. But that is not a term of derogation. Rather, it's an honor to be a control person. They are the movers and shakers...the ones who get things done...the leaders in all phases of our life. So, I love myself exactly as I am! I was determined to build a home on the lot that I bought... and I did.

We bought the lot from a Realtor who was a daughter of Clair Pearson, a bridge friend in Decatur. She was a lovely woman, who helped us a lot. She took us to see two model homes on Longboat Key. We liked the one built by a friend of hers, Bill McGinnis. She recommended him highly as a quality builder and he was the one we hired for our project. Two things struck us as outstanding in Bill's model home: the vaulted ceiling and the Mexican tile. Of course, we were just looking around, because some day, in the distant future, we might consider moving to Sarasota permanently.

NEXT CHAPTER: I get hot and M/GM gets hotter.

MUCH LOVE,

❏ Dad    ❏ G.P.

# Chapter XV
# Sarasota
# The Early Days — 2

In Chapter XIV, I wrote that I got hot and your M/GM got hotter. Let me explain. Some of you will remember that I made an office for myself out of the former recreation room at the west side of the basement. It was quite nice with carpeting, desks, files, and a telephone extension.

I got hot on the phone by calling Bill McGinnis in Sarasota. He's an excellent builder, whom I had hired (without M/GM's knowledge) to build our home in Sarasota. It seems that your M/GM didn't trust me because she started to listen to my conversations when she picked up the phone upstairs.

Then came the confirmation: "What's this about ground elevation, room sizes, and building costs?" I was cornered and had to confess to my nefarious plotting and planning for our new home in Sarasota.

Then, your M/GM got HOTTER! She said, "In that case, let's fly down to Sarasota and do it right!" We did that in July 1977. It was 95° in Sarasota as we got off the plane on the ground. We almost went back home. But, we had a great visit with the architect and Bill McGinnis. We made a few changes in the plans that were already drawn up and signed an agreement to build as soon as possible.

Our next trip to Sarasota was in October. We found that dirt had been piled on the site to meet elevation requirements and the entire slab was poured with its plumbing and other factors built into it. Our good friend, Lou Simpson, who lived nearby was my chief inspector. He told me he came every day to check the progress. Oddly enough, building was begun simultaneously with ours on the lot across the street and the lot that one. They had all been vacant lots for twenty years.

We chose Sarah Paver to help us with the decorating. She, too, was a friend of our Realtor. Sarah was an outspoken, salty person and we had a great time with her working out the color scheme for the drapes, carpet and furniture. After we lived in the house for a few years, we worked with Ann Folsom Smith, an excellent designer, and we completed the job. It was so good, the house looks the same today.

The house was finished just in time for our 40th anniversary on April 4th, 1978. At that time we had carpeting on the floor and the drapes were hung...no furniture. So we did what we always do: had a party to celebrate both events.

We invited about forty or fifty people...old friends, bridge friends, and the builder and his crews. We hired a well-known caterer who brought in tables and chairs, and an excellent chicken dinner. Price was no object, as she charged the large sum of $10.00 per person. We came across the bill recently.

Coinciding with our party were the Academy Awards. That inspired me to have the "Blue Jay" Awards. I found an excellent artist who drew a beautiful blue jay, which was placed at the top of the award which was printed on an 8x11 certificate like a diploma. Then we made awards to "Best Contractor," "Best Designer," "Best Foreman," "Best Landscaper," etc. The biggest award went to your M/GM. She was honored as "Best Wife." It was really a fun evening...my first in Sarasota.

We moved from Decatur in July 1978 with all our furniture, Barbie, Nudgie, and Donna. Barbie hated the hot weather...her long hair was designed for cold weather. Nudgie and Donna loved it. They never went outside, and they had a huge new home to romp in.

Your M/GM was fifty-nine years old shortly after we got here and I was sixty-two. That sounds so young!! Your M/GM was the cook, a job she had for twenty years. She immediately got involved with Sisterhood at Temple Emmanuel and other organizations and played a lot of bridge.

I still owned the store and worked with Roger by phone. I was the President of Lincoln Manor and ran it by phone. We also had the property on N. Main Street, which needed a lot of management. Also, I too played a lot of bridge...once a bridge bum, always a bridge bum.

A year after we moved to Sarasota, an event of great importance took place. It was your M/GM's 60th birthday. I decided to have a "surprise" party for her. I invited Rabbi Opher and his wife and a large group of friends from Temple Emmanuel. We also had bridge friends and others...almost sixty in all. I told your M/GM that we'd go out for dinner with Lou and Deena Simpson. Deena's job was to keep M/GM in her bedroom, while all the guests, who had come in through the garage, were assembled in the living room. When they came out of the bedroom, they were greeted by an off-key version of "Happy Birthday to You." She was really surprised and it was another successful party. You can't beat good food and plenty of booze!

NEXT CHAPTER: Chapter XVI - My Federation Years

MUCH LOVE,

❏ Dad     ❏ G.P.

# Chapter XVI — The Sarasota-Manatee Jewish Federation and Me

First of all, I want to tell you that Jewish Federations have done a fantastic job of raising funds for Jewish charities, both here and abroad. They are umbrella organizations for all local Jewish organizations and, by giving money to a U.J.A. they have assisted thousands of desperate Jews reach Israel, and help them financially until they are established. In every major (even minor) city, money is distributed every year to the local J.C.C., Jewish Family Service and Senior Housing.

Others can help the very worthwhile groups such as United Charities, Red Cross, etc., but only Jews give to the Federations. My fondest hope is that all of you will contribute generously every year to your local Federations.

We had no Federation in Decatur - too small. But we did raise money every year for the UJA (United Jewish Appeal). Your M/GM was the Treasurer and I was a Solicitor. So, it was only natural for me to offer my services to the "Drive" in Sarasota. They gave me the cards for Bird Key which was quite different. Most of the Jews on Bird Key were quite reticent about giving. They hadn't been trained properly.

At that time, the Jewish population was only four to five thousand and the Federation was quite small. The office was on the second floor at 1900 Main Street - two small rooms. It was there that I met a man who would become a very close friend. Jack Weintraub had come here for an interview to replace Florence Sinclair as Executive Director. We liked him; we hired him. That was the beginning of the rapid growth of our Federation. I didn't mention that I was on the Board of Directors.

To take care of an expanded organization, we moved to larger quarters on Ringling Boulevard - on the first floor!

I was elected President in 1984 and served for two years. I'm patting myself on the back, but it's true: these were two years of exceptional growth. We had to get a bigger office or build our own building. I proposed the latter to the Executive Committee with the promise that I would chair the Capital Fund Committee. They took me up on my offer and we raised all the money and built the building on McIntosh.

Shortly after we moved to the new building, Jack Weintraub came to me and said that Hirsch Freed was willing to give a rather large sum to name the J.C.C., which we needed. Again, the Board voted to have a Capital Fund Drive, and again I chaired that committee. Everyone was quite enthusiastic, because we realized that our Jewish population would burgeon (which it did) and we needed proper facilities. We built the J.C.C., this time with a mortgage, and it was expanded a few years ago.

Jerry Engman was the Chairman of the Jewish Family and Children's Committee. He came to me in 1985 and said, "Gersh, we need a real J.F.C.S., not a committee. Our social worker, Millie Rostow, does little more than refer people to local agencies." Once again, the Executive Committee and Board voted to establish a J.F.C.S. with staff and their own office. Today they have a lovely building and large staff. "Great oaks from little acorns grow."

In the same period, the early eighties, Jerry Kapner and David Anchin pushed hard, and got, a Jewish Foundation. I was not involved in its inception, but served on the initial Board. I also used the Foundation for our Philanthropic Fund and our MAJOR Charitable Trust, which was set up for twenty years. That time will be up in December, just five years from now.

I have covered all the major Jewish institutions except one... the Jewish Housing Council. That is a story of its own which will be told in Chapter XVII

MUCH LOVE,  ❏ Dad  ❏ G.P.

# Chapter XVII
# The Jewish Housing Council and Me

As I remember, it was the fall of 1986. Your M/GM and I were in our car after leaving Sudakoff Hall where two Brandeis professors had led some wonderful discussions. We couldn't move because Marie Brown came dashing toward the car and in a loud, somewhat accusatory voice, said "What's happening with Senior Housing?" I replied, "Don't ask me. I'm not the President of the Jewish Federation now. Ask Eddie Shapiro. He's my successor."

Here's a little background to the problem of Jewish Senior Housing. It had been discussed for years. Rabbi Albert and Rose Shulman headed group discussions on the subject a long time ago and every Federation President had a committee which was completely powerless, because no one was interested in raising money for the project and there was little interest in the Jewish community for senior housing.

I can recall appointing a committee headed by Bernie Rothlein, and thinking to myself that they would talk and talk and nothing would happen. I was right.

So, when Marie went to Ed Shapiro with the problem, he did what any good president did: he formed a committee, with Marie's help and of course, made Marie the chairman.

It was an excellent committee! Besides Marie and me, were Jack Weintraub, who had recently resigned as Executive Director of the Federation, Jerry Engman, a businessman from Illinois, Jerry Kapner, who had preceded me as President of the Federation. Henry Steinhaus, who had built and operated nursing homes in Kansas, and Abe Horn. I had met Abe several years previously and got him interested in helping the Jewish community. He was a successful engineer and builder, and he had supervised the building of the J.C.C. as I had requested.

Later, we added Saul Chernowitz, which prompted your M/GM to call our group "Snow White and the Seven Dwarfs." As the years went by, we added Marty Lipton, who helped Abe Horn with the building and Max Bussel, a CPA, who helped in our financing.

This committee was different from the ones that preceded it. We were truly serious about building after we had studied the problem carefully. We felt there was great need for independent living and assisted care facilities for both our growing elderly population and relatives of our younger people. We were proven right on both counts.

When our conclusions were presented to the Executive Committee and Board of Federation, with the request for financial involvement, we were turned down. They were too short-sighted and feared financial ruin.

This prompted the three businessmen, Jerry Engman, Henry Steinhaus, and me, all of whom had built with little or no money, to say, "We don't need the Federation. We can do it ourselves!!" Everyone agreed...and we were on our way.

We were very businesslike in our approach. I was the fund raiser (what else?) and I raised "seed money" by calling a meeting at our home of people whom I felt would help financially. I really don't remember them all but I do remember Harold Slosberg and Paul Klingenstein. We all put up $10,000 knowing full well that it might not be successful. I think it was $70,000 - $80,000 in the first meeting. When we ran out of money, I went back to the same people and got more. We were so confident that no one thought of failure.

We made Jack Weintraub the Executive Director at the princely sum of $1,000 a month. We rented a small office and met every week for seven years. Our chief discussions were (1) property, (2) finance, (3) fundraising, and (4) building design.

There wasn't a single piece of decent property we didn't check out. We were honest with the owners: if they wanted to sell us their property, they'd have to wait until we got our loan to get paid. This precluded a lot of good locations, but we plowed along. The twenty-nine acres that we finally bought was negotiated unsuccessfully originally. But we were most fortunate. The owner went bankrupt and the bank in charge of asset liquidation agreed to sell to us with the proviso above. We have some wonderful, positive men who made everyone confident that our mission was do-able.

"Building Deisgn" was in the capable hands of Abe Horn who had help from Marty Lipton and Saul Chernowitz. We hired Mike Ritter as our architect and we all participated in discussion of the structure of Kobernick House. It turned out well.

When I speak of finances, I mean the major loan or loans we needed. John Haylett was hired as financial advisor. He was a wonderful man who was well versed in major financing, and he agreed to wait for our loan to be made before being paid. He, too, had confidence in us.

Fundraising was my job and it was difficult. The Jewish community had interest in the project, but they were unwilling to give…especially money. The Federation considered us competition for the Jewish money and, as a result, NOT ONE OFFICER OR BOARD MEMBER gave us a penny. A friend who attended an Executive committee meeting heard the Executive Director of the Federation say, "Don't worry about them, they'll never make it." One lady of means was initially interested and offered us $75,000. With a little persuasion on my part, she doubled it. Then I offered her the naming of the building for $300,000 and she did it. She was Gail Kobernick…and liked the ring of "KOBERNICK HOUSE" which I proposed.

David Anchin and I each put up $75,000 to name two of the three wings. But the third was Marie Brown's big surprise. She didn't know, until we opened, that the third wing was named for her. I got $25,000 from an old boyfriend of hers, a wealthy Texas oil man, and the other $50,000 from her local friends.

Other major gifts were the "Milter" dining room and the "Slosberg" Bistro. There were many small gifts, or course, but our final total was a paltry

$1,200,000. Hardly enough for a $25,000,000 building.

So, I dreamed up another approach: bonds. We sold bonds in lots of $5,000 or $10,000 and we were honest. We told prospects that we'd pay 9%, but they were "Z" rated. However, they'd be helping the project. Marie and Jack and I went into homes where people gathered to see and hear our "dog and pony show." It worked...about as good as our fundraising... roughly $900,000 was sold.

John Haylett had his hands full. With only $1,200,000 in cash and $900,000 in bond sales (a debt) it was difficult to interest prospective lenders. We did have the county muni-bond classification, which had an appeal as a muni "junk bond." He got PRUDENTIAL and VAN CAMPEN MERRITT to come down to visit us. They were tremendously impressed by the quality of our Board, the need for our project, and our Jewish community and they agreed to do it as a joint venture.

When they came down to dot the "i's" and cross the "t's" before signing, their hot shot lawyer, Walter Diutch, put the screws to us. He added a number of clauses that we didn't like because they added more cost. But, we had to agree to them. Thus, when I introduced him to my wife at the celebration dinner that evening, she said, in her inimitable way, "Oh, you're the momser (S.O.B.) who gave us such a hard time." This, of course, went down in the history of the Housing Council.

Because of my involvement with my eyes and the many procedures involved, I was not a key factor in the planning and building of the assisted care facility. When the fundraising was agreed, I insisted that Jack Weintraub be the chairman. I agreed to help him and got the major gift of $500,000 from Ann Anchin. I also had a plan which worked: we asked people of means for $50,000. Sanford Milter and I helped Jack with this phase, and we raised enough cash to be able to issue the muni-bonds that were needed.

We went to Kobernick House this week for dinner and a show to celebrate the 10th Anniversary since its dedication. Ethel Bieber wrote the show and it was great! She made parodies of many popular songs extolling the virtues of living at Kobernick House. So much has happened in the past ten years... most of it good. There has been a rapprochement between the Federation and the Housing Council. We have been an agency of the Federation for many years, and we receive money from them every year. Those actively engaged in running the Federation, board and staff, and their counterparts in the Housing Council get along well. In fact, our present President, Ken Stock, came from their board to ours and he has done an outstanding job.

There are two other positive factors: (1) the Jewish Community now has warm feelings for Anchin and Kobernick and our donor base broadened and (2) we reached a turning point financially, with the first month of positive cash flow. This is due to the addition of apartments at Anchin and effective expense control. With over $30,000,000 in bonds out-standing, it will be a long time before we are free of debt. But I have every confidence that this Jewish community, and the Jewish Housing Council will prevail.

When I look back over the years we spent on these two edifices, the odds that were against us, and the absolute MIRACLE that we wrought, I have to conclude that this was the greatest project that I ever worked on.

It was most meaningful because of the positive spirit of cooperation of all the Board members. There were differences of opinion, but never a harsh word, never dissension.

And, when I visit Kobernick and Anchin and see how many personal friends and so many others have benefited from our hard work, I KVELL, yes I really KVELL!!

# Chapter XVIII
# Parties in Sarasota

I probably won't remember all the parties we had in Sarasota, when we were young and enjoyed giving parties. Now your M/GM doesn't even want to have two people over for dinner. "Let's take them out to a restaurant," she says.

Our first party was our 40th anniversary in April 1978. I wrote all about that one a few chapters ago. If you'll recall, all we had in the house was carpeting and drapes...no furniture.

In the ensuing few years, we had a number of welcome parties for new Jewish residents under the sponsorship of the Federation.

Do you remember Connie Mack, the senator from Florida? His grandfather owned and managed the old Philadelphia A's baseball team and he (the grandfather) was a known anti-Semite. Also Connie Mack was a REPUBLICAN. This caused great concern among our Jewish friends, when we hosted a party for him when he was running for the Senate. Your M/GM said to the naysayers "look, he should get to know us and our wishes."

As usual, she was right! The big questions that were asked were about his attitude toward Israel. He told us he knew little about Israeli affairs but promised to look into it. He did, and he became one of the biggest supporters of Israel in Congress. Again M/GM was right!

I think I wrote about M/GM's 60th birthday party when she came out of our bedroom ostensibly to go out for dinner, but instead found sixty people in the house singing "Happy Birthday." Her sixty-fifth was a dandy, too. We called it her "Medicare" birthday and that was the theme of the evening. It was held at the Four Winds restaurant on Longboat Key. We took it over for the night. Great food... French cuisine... with the best pecan pies I ever tasted. It's gone now.

Most of you were with us on her next three major birthdays:   70th Caribbean cruise with family, 75th trip to Hawaii with family (four condos and four cars) and the 80th family trip to Alaska where we toured and cruised.

There were lots of dinner parties for different occasions, but there were two that I remember well.  They were January 1st and 2nd to celebrate the New Year.  The weather was warm and we ate on the lanai.  It was two consecutive days so that we could have all the friends we wanted to join us in ushering in the New Year.

Perhaps our greatest party, from the standpoint of originality and execution, was what I called the "Bad Taste" party.  I stated in the invitation that no one would be admitted with regular clothes.  All dress was to be in bad taste.  Well, it was a large crowd and the costumes were truly outlandish. We all laughed and laughed at what were truly original "wrong" things to wear to a party.  Our neighbor across the street, Anita Sulek, won first prize.  She wore her bridal dress.

Our 50th Anniversary party was held at the Longboat Key Club.  Many of you were there and can attest to its warmth and happiness.  We have two videos of it in our collection to prove it.   M/GM/GGM was here and we celebrated her 95th birthday at the Colony – another lovely affair.  There we met Phil Mancini, a 21-year-old man who handled the party for the Colony.   He was quite taken with M/GM, but  he told her, "the next time you see me, I'll be at Michael's and I'll be more expensive."  It's true.  He and Michael Klauber set up a dining hall and catering business that has been amazingly successful.  Phil and I worked out the details of our party on June 14th last year. He told me, "I'll be there myself to see that everything runs smoothly." He did and it did!!

A few years ago your M/GM was asked by Brandeis Women to host a fundraiser in our home. She agreed, but Stan and I did all the work. We set up chairs for sixty women to enjoy a string quartet in our living room, and tables and chairs for all sixty to enjoy a lunch afterwards. We served twenty inside and forty on the lanai. This was so successful that it was repeated the following year. That was followed the next year with a concert only...no food...and since then... NADA.

I really and truly enjoyed my 80th birthday. Almost all of you were there... at Michael's on East... and I called it a "Roast." Jerry Roucher was an excellent M.C. and the "roasters" did a great job. It's all on video...very funny.

Our 60th Anniversary party was, to some, a comparatively small, intimate affair. About fifty people... all the room would hold...at the old Radisson. I called this one a tribute to your M/GM and I had the pleasure of being the M.C. Somebody said, after seeing the video, that I talked too much. That was probably true, but he (or she) forgot that I was entitled. It was my bill!

I think you'll all agree that I outdid myself on June 12th, 13th, and 14th last year as a combination family reunion and 65th Anniversary party. With E.J.'s help, everyone was seated properly and everything went smoothly. It was truly wonderful!!! But, as I announced at the time: THAT'S THE LAST OF OUR PARTIES. I hope I'm wrong!

# Chapter XIX
# The Odyssey of
# Odysseys — Part 1

I think I wrote about our trip to Israel in 1979. Here it is in greater detail. There were thirty-five to forty of us, all members of Temple Emanuel. Rabbi Opher was our leader and, since he had lived in Israel for the first thirty years of his life, he was a fantastic guide. He took us many places that tourists don't see as well as all the regular stops. He was born and reared in Sephat which is now an artist colony. We visited all his old haunts.

After ten days in Israel, a few of us took a side trip to Egypt. Because Egypt and Israel were at odds then, we had to fly to Greece first, and then to Egypt. We spent a lot of time with Harold and Helen Lyons who were good tourists. "Let's see it all" was our motto.

One night the four of us went to a nightclub which was on top of a building that tilted like the Tower of Pisa. We went up a rickety elevator, hoping it would work, and ordered a beer each. It came in quart bottles, which made us very happy.

In Cairo we visited the old city, and the area where Jews had lived. In an old synagogue, we had a long talk with the "Shamus." He liked me so much he was going to sell me the Torah for a small sum, since they had no services anymore. One of his friends came by and stopped the transaction.

We loved the pyramids... wondered if the slaves who built them were Jewish. It was simply amazing that they were built to such exacting specifications without our modern methods or machinery. We went up a ladder in one of them to a platform in the exact center. From there it was equal distance in length in every direction.

We all became so close on this trip that we decided to meet once a year and we did until two years ago. We called the group "The Mishpocha" and those of us who are still living are good friends.

In 1982 we took a cruise on the STELLA SOLARIS, a small ship that took us to some wonderful stops in Turkey and Greece. We loved Istanbul, especially the Grand Bazaar. I don't remember what we bought the girls, but I do remember buying a light green soft leather jacket for David.

One of the spectacular sights, for me, was seeing Mykonos, a Greek city built on a hill. All of the roofs and buildings are white and the houses are close together. As we came to the port, we saw this mass of white roofs and buildings.

We saw palaces and churches in both Greece and Turkey... also a lot of ruins of old buildings. It was a revelation to both of us to see the activity in these faraway places that were so important in our early civilization.

One of our greatest trips was the "Grand Tour of Yugoslavia." I have never met anyone, before or after this trip, who had been on it. This two week tour was inexpensive, complete, and wonderful.

We flew to Belgrade, where the tour started. I think it was in 1983, just after the end of Tito's rule. It was ironic, in light of the recent breakup of Yugoslavia and the wars, that the first thing the guide showed us in the park at Belgrade was a building that housed statues representing each of the six provinces. She bragged about how well these diverse groups got along. It must have been the power of the dictator, Tito. It was still a communist country, but we never saw a policeman.

I remember traveling to Mostar, famous for its unique bridge, which was destroyed in the war. Then, there was Sarejavo, which was famous because it was there that World War I began. The best stop was Dubrovnik, the Miami Beach of Yugoslavia. We spent three days there, basking in the sun and touring the city.

We spent time in many cities such as Split and Zagreb. I loved the small town of Lubliana, where we were surprised to find a department store.

But I love the name itself. Repeat it several times, Lubliana, Lubliana, Lubliana.

The tour wound up where it started - Belgrade. We had a night on our own... the plane for the U.S. was the next day... so we decided to go to the Opera. We had dinner in the hotel, went outside to get a streetcar to take us downtown to the Opera. We jumped on as it was leaving and hung on until we got downtown. It was so crowded we never saw a conductor and thus didn't pay.

Outside the Opera House were large photos of the famous diva who was performing that night. She was Russian, and obviously quite famous. After the first act, your M/GM said "There's something wrong. The Russian singer sounds so different from the rest." We found out later that she was singing in Russian, while the rest of the cast and the chorus sang in Yugoslavian. The entire experience of the opera in Belgrade was exciting to two young enterprising Americans.

And – the Grand Tour of Yugoslavia was truly GRAND for us!!

# Chapter XX
# The Odyssey of Odysseys — Part 2

## 1983 PORTUGAL, SPAIN, MOROCCO

In 1983, four wonderful people... Arlene, Vicki, your M/GM and I, went to explore the denizens of those three countries. We were in Lisbon, Ronde, Fez, Toledo, Malaga, Seville, Marakesh, Rabat, and Tangiers. And... I have pictures in an album to prove it.

One of our greatest adventures was seeing Gibraltar. It is an impressive sight. But the highlight of the trip was Casablanca. It was a revelation to see this city that became so notorious because of the film. I shall never forget the night we were there. Arlene (she is the shy one) said, "Look, it's a balmy night in glorious Casablanca... with a full moon... I wish I had a man!"

It was quite wonderful to see how people lived in those countries. The bazaar in Marakesh was spectacular. It was there that I bought two large handmade plates for $50.00 each. To keep them intact, I "schlepped" them through airports all the way home... they were heavy, too. I gave one away... the other is hanging on the wall as you approach the "girls bedroom." It is quite ugly.

## 1984 NORTHWEST UNITED STATES, CANADA, CANADIAN ROCKIES

There were twenty of us in this Westtour two week trip. The group was so small that we became fast friends for the duration.

We started in Montana where we visited small towns like Jasper and Kalis Pell. We saw the Grand Coulee Dam, St. Mary's Lake, Glacier National

Park and lots of mountains... all very impressive.

In the Canadian Rockies, we also saw plenty of mountains, snow, and rivers. We actually walked on a glacier, and your M/GM - more venturesome than I - went down the Alabaster River on a raft. Banff, on Lake Louise was especially lovely, as well as a huge waterfall on the Bow River.

We stopped briefly in a lot of small towns, but we really enjoyed two large ones, Calgary and Victoria. Both of these cities had fantastic gardens. Although Victoria Gardens are well known, we thought the Calgary Gardens were just as spectacular.

In one of those cities, we saw Madame Toussant's Wax Museum and we got a kick out of visiting Parliament while it was in session in Victoria.

I must confess: my memory of this tour was jogged by the beautiful pictures in our album!

# 1987 HONG KONG, TAIWAN, GUADALCANAL, CHINA, KOREA

This was a sight-seeing cruise on the Princess Line, with stops in all these countries. We flew to Hong Kong and spent two days in amazement at the sophistication of that city. Then we sailed to Taiwan, which also was impressive because they seemed so industrious and productive.

The main stop was China, but because China was at odds with the Chinese who had set up competition on Taiwan, we couldn't sail directly to China. Thus, the stop at the island of Guadalcanal in between. However, because of its significance in WWII, we found Guadalcanal very interesting.

Then, we sailed to Shanghai, a large bustling city. I think I wrote about this before, but it bears repeating. A bus took us to visit a school. As we came to a stop, a beautiful little girl made eye contact with your M/GM through the window of the bus. When we got off, she was waiting for your M/GM and gave her a private tour of the school. That's called "instant charisma."

We went by bus to Beijing where the first stop was Tiananmen Square. It's the largest square in the world... simply huge. This, of course, is where the protestors for human rights were battled a few years ago.

The Great Wall of China was the main bus stop. It was wonderful! Your M/GM stopped at a resting place, while I went on a mile or two further. When I returned, I found her in deep conversation with a tall handsome Chinese young man. He told us he wanted to come to the U.S. to study at HAAHD. I first thought of Howard University, but then realized that he meant Harvard. He was very nice and quite bright.

Incidentally, we met a lovely young couple on this cruise who were on their honeymoon. They were Maria and Allen Bleicher, and I interject them now because of an incident at Seoul, Korea.

We all had a ball at the Bazaar in Seoul. There I purchased a white jacket for $5.00 and six to eight all-cotton golf shirts for $3.00 each. Allen Bleicher said that they were so inexpensive we could wear them a few years and then use them to wash the car. That was 1987.

I think I'll call Allen and tell him I still use the jacket every winter and have two of the shirts left. In fact, I'm wearing one now!!

# Chapter XXI
# The Odyssey of
# Odysseys — Part 3

I didn't realize how much we had traveled until I went into my memory bank and the voluminous pictures I took and put into albums. There were several trips to England where we enjoyed visiting Hazel and Geoff Pollard and their family. We also had several Caribbean cruises and trips to Mexico.

Elderhostel was an important source for travel and education. I shall never forget the "Hollywood Bowl" trip with a full course in music appreciation. The most memorable Elderhostel trip took us to a small college in the Carmel Valley. At the time we went, the weather was so PERFECT wonderful that I thought it was the Garden of Eden.

But there is one odyssey that is head and shoulders above all the others, and that is my subject today. It was the trip with Vicki and Howard, Sarah and Loren, Tanya and Justin... David, Jean, and Molly couldn't make it and Arlene had broken her leg. This was a wild two week trip with overnight stops in Zagreb, Venice, Padua, St. Moritz, Salzburg, Budapest, Vienna, and Belgrade.

We started in Zagreb, Yugoslavia, and were delighted to find that tour bus... a brand new Mercedes Benz... was complete with a driver, Nevin, our guide and no other travelers. This was the height of luxury. We surmised that no one else wanted a trip with so many stops.

In Yugoslavia we visited some huge caves. Vicki said these caves... which were truly enormous... are her greatest remembrances of the trip. Also, in Yugoslavia we went to the winter home of the Lipizzaner horses. Your M/GM loves animals and petted one of the horses in the stable. He promptly bit her. Must have been anti-Semitic! We went to a doctor who fixed her up without a fee. Socialized medicine was a wonderful legacy left by

Tito.

The high spot for me was Venice. The canals, of course, were spectacular, but the highlight of the trip was a visit with Lino Tagliapietra and his wife on the island of Murano, where all the glass blowers live and work. Lino was a friend of Howard's and he had made a date (before the visit) to take them out to lunch.

Lino was considered one of the best glass blowers in the world. When Howard was the Director of Haystack, Lino taught glass blowing there. He and his wife were extremely warm and friendly. They greeted us as if we were family, and wouldn't consider eating out. They gave us one of the best meals we ever had.

After lunch we went to Lino's shop, where he put on an exhibition of glass blowing. It was truly exciting. I bought a vase that he had for sale... today it's worth about ten times what I paid because Lino's work is so valuable.

Sarah's baggage had been lost by the airline. This gave her and G.P. a time of "togetherness" as they bought UNDERWEAR for her in Venice.

We stayed overnight in Venice and on our way north, we stopped in Padua and Verona, (Tanya's Shakespeare cities). Then, to St. Moritz in Switzerland, where we stayed overnight. I must confess that I remember everything about this trip except Switzerland. Howard thinks it's because I was a little pale as we negotiated the zigzag narrow road as we drove slowly up the Alps.

The next major stop was Salzburg, Austria but on the way we had lunch in Liechtenstein. That was a little lilting lesson in alliteration.

Salzburg was impressive. We split up on the tours there. Some of us saw the sights in the city, while others went to the "Sound of Music" country. They saw all the wonderful hills that had been "alive with music."

Austria was like its name, "austere." We loved its "old world" elegance. There was one huge jarring note in Vienna. The four youngsters, traveling on their own, saw a number of anti-Semitic comments on the bulletin in the Grand Opera House.

Budapest was beautiful with the Blue Danube flowing between the cities of Buda and Pest. We learned that these cities were once separate entities.

After Budapest, we drove through Czechoslovakia on our way to Belgrade, Yugoslavia. This was our disembarking city.

We had been… in two weeks… in eight countries: Yugoslavia, Italy, Switzerland, Germany (one corner of it), Liechtenstein, Austria, Hungary, and Czechoslovakia.

As I review this trip, I conclude that it was so special for many reasons. First, the luxury of a brand new bus, with driver and guide all to ourselves. Secondly, the wonderful stops that were all so steeped in history… and so beautiful. Thirdly, the fantastic camaraderie among the eight of us, and fourthly, the sheer enjoyment shared by all of us for two weeks. We shared our love of travel and our love for one another. It was truly a lovely and loving experience.

# Chapter XXII
# The Odyssey of
# Odysseys — Part 4

It is fitting that this is the final chapter on the odysseys, because I'm going to write briefly about our family trips on your M/GM's major birthdays.

If you'll recall, I told you about the surprise party we had here in our home for her 60th. And, the big "Medicare" party at the "4 Winds" restaurant for her 65th. When the 70th was approaching, your M/GM said to me, "We've had enough parties on my major birthdays. Let's take our immediate family on a trip!" I said, "That's a great idea. We'll do it!" And we did.

We all took a Caribbean cruise on her 70th birthday... that is, all but David, Jean, and Molly. Molly was one year old and D and J felt it would be too difficult for her.

We had numerous stops, where we'd take tours of the island of choice, plus snorkeling on the beaches for the older four grandchildren. The Caribbean is a wonderful place for relaxation. Combine that with the marvelous food and drinks on the ship, and you have a bunch of happy campers saying that this is a wonderful way to celebrate a major birthday. As the British say, "Well done!"

When her 75th birthday rolled around, we were delighted that six-year-old Molly and her poppa and mama could join us to make it a complete family affair. David secured a package deal on the island of Maui in Hawaii. It included our transportation, four condominiums, and four automobiles. It combined "togetherness" and "apartness" in just the right amounts, as we all made our own breakfasts in our individual condos, then spent the day jointly or separately as we enjoyed exploring the sights and wonders of Maui. Molly loved spending time with "the big kids" and they didn't feel put upon when she joined them.

Arlene and I took a helicopter trip which traveled all around the area. She says she has a video of that trip. Another unusual experience several of us enjoyed was going down in a submarine. And of course, there were miles and miles of glorious beaches. And the pineapples... I think most of them were grown on Maui.

Our "apartness" ended every night as we got together to enjoy the savory elegance of wonderful restaurants. David selected some and I picked some.

Now comes the biggie... the 80th... over three-fourths of a century. We chose Alaska - "well done" again. This trip was so fabulous because we not only had a marvelous time, but we learned so much about this unusual state.

We all flew from our home cities to Fairbanks, where we took a train to Denali National Forest. On the way, we sat in observation cars and looked out at the wildlife of Alaska as we enjoyed our dinner.

For me, Denali was the high spot of the trip. As we toured we saw so many different animals and the views were great. In the background was Mt. Everest Does he mean Denali?. This mountain was called "Denali" by the Indians. Before I got that information, I thought the park was named after an Italian explorer.

There were smaller mountains in the park... Justin and Tanya climbed to the top of one while some of us descended down a steep incline to see a lake. It's impossible to describe such natural beauty.

From Denali we traveled by train again to Anchorage. We toured this interesting city and then took what is called an "Alaskan Cruise" with four ports of call: Juneau, Ketchikan, Skagway, and Vancouver, Canada.

I forgot to mention that we had a wonderful addition to our family... Barbara...who was a big help to Sarah and me, taking your M/GM around the city of Juneau. Our cab driver was well-informed and so were we after he took us to see most of the interesting sights.

Ketchikan was a quaint old city. My biggest memory there is going into a tavern and asking for draft beer. The bartender sent me to the hotel down the street. I not only got the beer, but I also received a visual explanation of the small brewery. I believe this was the time where we stood on a bridge and watched the salmon as they were swimming upstream to spawn.

Skagway was like an old western town. This was one of the towns that participated in the big gold rush. We saw a creek where they panned the gold.

The inner passage was next. It's a huge body of water along the Alaskan coast that leads to Vancouver. There we tearfully said goodbye to one another. Some stayed to see Vancouver. Others flew home immediately. All of us left with a feeling of "mission accomplished." We celebrated 80 years of wonderful living by a wonderful woman in a wonderful, wonderful way.

# Chapter XXIII
# The 85<sup>th</sup> Birthday Party

There is no formal party for your M/GM but there will be a party in honor of this milestone event. Arlene, Vicki, and David are coming here in July at birthday time and we'll celebrate then, as well as every time one (or two) of you come to visit. We'll continue to drink toasts to a wonderful lady who has enhanced all our lives with her upbeat laugh and giggles.

She has made a big turnaround in the last week or two. We have a new doctor, a geriatric psychiatrist, but we've just seen him once. Vicki and I are convinced that this major change has been brought about by her weekly trips to her acupuncturist. These treatments will continue indefinitely!

As we get older, we're inclined to review the past...with all its pluses and minuses. We (your M/GM and I) have come to conclude that our greatest contribution to mankind has been our three children and five grandchildren, all of whom are dedicated to improving the lot of their fellow man. We have compiled this list for your edification:

ARLENE - Social Justice For All
SARAH - Our #1 Environmentalist
BARBARA - Acupuncture Teacher and Practitioner
LOREN - Teacher, the "Noblest Profession"
PATTY - Mother of the Greatest Great-Grandchild Ever
VICKI - Acupuncture Teacher and Practitioner
HOWARD - Acupuncture Teacher and Practitioner
TANYA & WILL - Our only Ph.D.'s and the very best Professors in New York and New Jersey
JUSTIN - Environmentalist and Savior of the World
DAVID - Zen Priest and Hospice Volunteer
JEAN - Helper for the Homeless
MOLLY - Future UNICEF President - Serving Children throughout the World

After reviewing the above listing, we are truly proud of all of you and your achievements, as we bask in the reflected glory.

# Chapter XXV
# The Penultimate Chapter

Chapter XXVI will be written by Loren, my chronicler, because at that time your M/GM and I will be safely ensconced in our last home in the burial ground of Temple Beth Israel. I write this without sadness. All our lives are finite and, although I'd like to live forever, I cannot. Perhaps we can live a little longer in your memories.

Enough of these happy thoughts. Let's talk about my plans for the rest of my life. Actually, it will be a sort of humdrum and repetitive existence. But, it's our life and we're happy with it.

There will be no (or very little) travel, but we'll enjoy the many visits from all of you. This gives us something to look forward to.

We'll also enjoy socializing with friends at small dinners here and at restaurants with close friends. We'll enjoy our relationships with Charlie and our STAFF: Stan, Ann, and E.J.

Of course, I'll have my bridge games to keep my mind sharp and my phone conversations with all of you and many others.

Hey! All that sounds pretty good!

Your M/GM has a sound body and she has no pain. We hope to maintain her present mental stability with proper medication and TLC. She tires easily and rests a lot.

I consider myself in excellent health for an 88-year-old man. I, too, tire easily and enjoy the naps that I take regularly.

I had a prostate operation twenty-three years ago and a four-way bypass thirteen years ago. Both have been exceptionally successful and have given me no trouble since I had them.

I almost forgot about my eyes. I have become so well-adjusted to being visually impaired that it seldom bothers me. That was not always the case. I remember clearly the conversation I had with Carol Cooperman, our neighbor, who was an excellent psychologist. She told me, after I had numerous eye procedures, that she recognized a lot of anger in my system. Having practiced "denial" all my life, I assured her that I was okay. "No, you're not," she said, "and I want you to consider group therapy with Paul White." He's the senior member of her group and had just organized a therapy group for men over seventy years of age. I decided to give it a try. It was one of the best decisions I ever made.

There were five of us in the group, each with a different problem. For example, one man wanted to work, but no one would hire him at his age. Another had very poor relations with his wife, etc., etc. The common thread was ANGER! We really helped each other a lot with our conversations and Paul White was always there to tie up loose threads as we went along.

I left the group after two years because I came to realize that my anger was more deep-seated….that I had really been angry all my life, and that I had a burning desire to know more about my psyche.

At this point, about six years ago, I sought the help of Vicki and Howard's therapist, Lynda Schmidt. I had been in counseling intermittently since I was thirty-five. Much of it was helpful, but I had never been able to get a true understanding of my inner feelings.

Yes, this is another one of my success stories…perhaps my greatest. Lynda is a marvelous therapist, and by using the mail, and mostly the phone, I have come to full knowledge of what makes me tick emotionally.

Besides the comfort of that knowledge, there has been a huge gain for me. My relationship with your M/GM has changed dramatically. The hallmark of the Woolf-Cohn family is ambivalence. My sister, Estelle, pointed that out to me many years ago. My mother and father had a love-hate relationship but it was covered completely by denial.

Your M/GM and I used to have this same kind of relationship without much denial. We fought a lot even though we loved one another. Now the negative factor is gone. We never fight, rarely argue, and live a wonderful, loving life together... which is what we both want.

I don't know how to end this penultimate chapter. Perhaps there is no ending... it will unfold (hopefully) over many years, until the final chapter is written.

We are grateful to Gersh for just being who he is and for offering so much to us all – his family, his friends, and his community.

May 20, 2011

Designed and produced in Blue Hill, ME
by
Merlin Design

http://merlin-design.net

Made in the USA
Charleston, SC
26 May 2011